Biblical Gardens of God and Valleys of Man

And the Lessons They Teach

Biblical Gardens of God and Valleys of Man

And the Lessons They Teach

by

Sylvia Bambola

Heritage Publishing House

For information contact:
Heritage Publishing House
heritagepubhouse@gmail.com

ISBN: 978-0-9657389-4-1

Unless otherwise indicated, all Scriptures taken from Holy Bible, King James version, Cambridge, 1769.

Also by Sylvia Bambola

Non-Fiction
Encountering Jesus Throughout the Bible
The Coming Deception
12 Questions New Christians Frequently Ask
Following the Blood Trail from Genesis to Revelation

Fiction:
Mercy at Midnight
The Babel Conspiracy
The Daughters of Jim Farrell
The Salt Covenants
Rebekah's Treasure
Return to Appleton
Waters of Marah
Tears in a Bottle
Refiner's Fire

To
My Children and Grandchildren
With Love

Table of Contents

Section One

Gardens of God

In this section, five gardens will be covered, along with the lessons they teach.

A garden is a place of beauty, refuge, and tranquility. It can also be a place of solitude and reflection, as well as a place of escape. Gardens can be secret. And some gardens are exclusive, meant only for the gardener's eyes. Other gardens are a source of food and nourishment.

In the Bible, the gardens of God tell a timeless story. They also reveal God's heart. It is here that He desires man to abide with Him.

The Garden of Eden

The Garden of Eden, **the garden of disobedience**, is the first garden in the Bible. It was a garden planted not by angels but by God Himself according to Genesis 2:8. *"And the LORD God planted a **garden** eastward in Eden."* It was a perfect paradise, a place where Adam and Eve met with God to walk and talk with Him in the cool of the day (Genesis 3:8). It was a place of joy and peace and beauty. It was also a place of protection until it became the garden of disobedience when Adam and Eve violated God's authority by wanting to become "as gods". The result: expulsion. Driven from the face of God and their beautiful paradise, life would forever be changed. Now, subjected to the elements of nature and hard labor in order to survive, man would face a new reality, the reality of adversity and sin.

Genesis 3:22-24 tells us what happened. *"And the LORD God said, Behold, the man is become as one of us* (the Trinity*) to know good and evil: and now, lest he put forth his hand, and take also of the tree of Life, and eat,* **and live for ever***: Therefore the LORD God sent him forth from the garden of Eden, to till the ground from whence he was taken. So he* (God) *drove out the man; and he placed at the east of the garden of Eden* **Cherubims***, and a flaming sword which turned every way, to keep the way of the tree of life."*

Note that God stationed powerful angels to prevent the banished couple from reentering Eden. These cherubims are the type of angels depicted at each end of the mercy seat on the ark of the covenant (Exodus 25:18-19). They are also the type of angels who, according to 2 Samuel 22:11 and Psalm 18:10, God rides upon. *"And he* (God) *rode upon a cherub and did fly and he was seen upon the wings of the wind."* And Psalm 99:1 tells us that God *"sitteth between the cherubims."*

God barring Eden was an act of judgment and of mercy. To prevent them from forever remaining in their fallen state, separated from Him, God had to keep Adam and Eve from eating of the tree of life. But He also had to deal with their grievous offense. Undoing it would

4

exact an enormous price. It would necessitate
two other gardens: the Garden of Gethsemane
and the Garden Tomb.

Sylvia Bambola

The Garden of Gethsemane

The garden of Gethsemane is **the garden of submission**. It was the first stop toward permanently correcting the damage done by Adam and Eve's sin. John 18:1 tells us it was the place where Jesus went after the last supper. *"When Jesus had spoken these words* (prayers to His Father to protect His disciples) *he went forth with his disciples over the brook Cedron, where was a garden, into the which he entered, and his disciples."*

Here, in agony of soul, Jesus sweated great drops of blood (Luke 22:44) after surrendering His will to that of the Father's. *"Not my will but thine be done,"* He said in Luke 22:42. He knew what was coming. The ordeal would be long and painful and crushing as the very weight of sin was placed upon Him. It is important to understand that without this surrender there would have been no crucifixion. Jesus could have called the whole thing off. But He didn't, and His surrender lead to another garden: the garden of death.

The Garden Tomb

The Garden Tomb is the **garden of death**. It was the place they buried Jesus after His submission in Gethsemane and subsequent trip to Golgotha. John 19:40-41 (Amplified) tells us, *"they took Jesus' body and bound it in linen cloths with the spices as is the Jews' customary way to prepare for burial. Now there was a **garden** in the place where He was crucified and in the **garden a new tomb**, in which no one had ever yet been laid."*

It's interesting to note that when Mary Magdalene saw Jesus for the first time as He stood near the empty tomb, John 20:15 tells us she thought He was the gardener. Words in the Bible are never wasted and often convey double meanings. Descriptions, too, are often types and foreshadows. In that context, Jesus *is* a gardener. With His blood, He paid the price for His seed, His future harvest, His bride, the very plantings that will go into His heavenly garden.

Isaiah 61:1-3 is a prophecy of Jesus' ministry and what He will accomplish. It's this very scripture or part of it (Isaiah 61:1-2a) that Jesus read in the synagogue after unrolling Isaiah's scroll and declaring Himself to be the Messiah. But in verse 3 it also says, *"To appoint unto them that mourn in Zion, to give unto them beauty for ashes, the oil of joy for mourning, the garment of praise for the spirit of heaviness; that they might be called **trees of righteousness, the planting of the LORD**, that he might be glorified."*

So, spiritually speaking, we are trees which our Heavenly Gardener, Jesus, plants. In turn, as trees of righteousness, we glorify Him. But the righteousness is all His which He imparts to us after we accept Him as Lord and Savior. How amazing!

In Mark 8:22-24, when Jesus healed the blind man, this occurred: *"And he* (Jesus) *cometh to Bethsaida; and they bring a blind man unto him, and besought him to touch him. And he took the blind man by the hand, and led him out of the town; and when he had spit on his eyes, and put his hands upon him, he asked him if he saw ought. And he* (the former blind man) *looked up and said, I see **men as trees walking**."* What happened? Did Jesus mess up?

Mark 8:25 goes on to say, *"After that* (after the man saw 'men as trees walking') *he* (Jesus) *put his hand again upon his eyes, and made him look up: and he was restored, and saw every man **clearly.**"*

No, Jesus didn't mess up. This was not an incomplete miracle, one that had to be redone in order to be corrected. Rather, Jesus first healed what was most important, the man's spiritual sight. Then Jesus restored his physical sight. It was the complete package. Indeed, that word "clearly" here means, "conclusion of an act, ray of light." The healing was concluded in two parts and involved light. Jesus is light itself; a light that not only gives spiritual enlightenment but lights the darkness; even the darkness caused by blindness both spiritual and physical.

Psalm 1 talks about the righteous as trees planted by the river and how they produce fruit in due season. *"And he* (the righteous) *shall be like a **tree** planted by the rivers of water, that bringeth forth his fruit in his season; his leaf also shall not wither; and whatsoever he doeth shall prosper."* Again, this is a picture of the believer as a tree, watered and nourished by God, and one who will produce fruit in proper season," (Psalm 1:3).

Sadly, we often vacillate between the garden of disobedience and the garden of submission. And what we find is that the garden of disobedience brings no joy, while the garden of submission, often difficult and gut wrenching, leads to the third garden, the garden of death— to the death of self. But it's the necessary path to the next two gardens: the Garden of Our Heart and the Garden of Heaven.

The Garden of our Heart

The beautiful garden of meeting. This garden is depicted in the Song of Solomon and is full of types and foreshadowing, with king Solomon representing Jesus as the bridegroom-king and the Shulamite woman representing Jesus' bride, the church. Indeed, Shulamite means, "peaceful, safe, complete, to be in a covenant of peace." It's a wonderful picture of the covenant position and benefits of believers.

Song of Solomon 4:12-16 portrays the garden, also a picture of the bride, this way: *"A **garden inclosed** is my sister, my spouse; a spring shut up, a fountain sealed. Thy plants are an orchard of pomegranates, with pleasant fruits; comphire, with spikenard, Spikenard and saffron; calamus and cinnamon, with all **trees** of frankincense; myrrh and aloes, with all the chief spices: A fountain of gardens, a well of living waters, and streams from Lebanon. Awake, O north wind; and come, thou south; blow* *upon my garden, that the spices thereof may flow out. Let my beloved come into his garden, and eat his pleasant fruits."*

God wants to make our heart His private garden. In ancient times, the king's garden was reserved for him alone. It was only for his use and pleasure, and not to be trampled by outsiders. In other words, it was exclusive. So, too, is this "inclosed" garden in Song of Solomon. It's private and only for the king's enjoyment. But because it is surrounded by an enclosure it also indicates both his protection, as well as chasteness on the part of the bride. He guards and tends it. She is exclusively his.

Notice how the king lavishes praise on his garden. He talks about its pleasant fruit and sweet-smelling spices, a place for him to come and enjoy its yield. In the same way, Jesus desires to come and enjoy the fruit in our garden, fruit that belongs to Him. It is the very fruit of the Holy Spirit planted in our heart for we are all His workmanship, the product of His labor.

Taking a closer look confirms this protection by the king. In Song of Solomon 4:12-16, that word "garden" is *gan,* a different word from the traditional word for garden, which is *ginnah,* and means just a garden or enclosure. *Gan,* on the other hand, means, "a garden, enclosure, to protect, defend." And it's the only word for garden used when referring to **the protective guardianship of God.** It implies that God has put a protective shield around this garden.

I like the Amplified version of verse 16: *"You have called me a garden, she* (the Shulamite woman) *said, Oh, I pray that the cold north wind* (symbol of adversity) *and the soft south wind may blow upon my garden, that its spices may flow out in abundance for you in whom my soul delights. Let my beloved come into his garden and eat its choicest fruits."* It's a picture indicating that a believer's life, even during times of adversity, should produce godly fruit and exude a pleasing fragrance for our King to enjoy.

In Song of Solomon 6:2, the bride, referring to the king going into his garden, says, *"My beloved is gone down to his **garden,** to the **beds** of **spices,** to **feed** in the gardens and to **gather lilies.**"*

The above provides a beautiful picture. "Beds" speak of a raised garden as well as something longed for. Spices speak of a sweet fragrance, something costly, a treasure. It represented one's wealth at that time. God considers us valuable. We are His treasure.

And feed is the word *raah* and speaks of tending a flock, pasture, to graze. It also means, "to be a friend of." In addition, it was used as a title of honor in royal names such as for kings. According to the *Theological Wordbook of the Old Testament*, in ancient times, rulers demonstrated their legitimacy to rule by their ability to "pasture their people." It reminds me of Psalm 23 (Amplified), *"The Lord is my Shepherd to feed, guide, and shield me, I shall not lack."* So, in this one word *"raah"* or "feed" we have a total word play showing Jesus as Shepherd, King, and Friend. WOW!

But there's more. As mentioned, Song of Solomon 6:2 tells us that the king went to his garden specifically to "gather lilies," and these two words give added insight. "Gather" means, "to gather or glean" and lilies mean, "flower, **whiteness, joy, and six-sided** (referring to the leaves of the lily)." Being six-sided symbolizes man, for six is the number of man. It's just another confirmation that we are the garden, the very ones Jesus takes pleasure in and looks to for fruits of righteousness.

The picture of the lily is a picture of our cleansed state, made white by King Jesus who died for us and redeemed us from the pit of sin and destruction. As cleansed and redeemed, we can be nothing but joyful, which is alluded to in the Hebrew definition of the lily. What joy to be free! What joy to know our future is secure! What joy to know we are so loved and cared for by our King! And what joy to know that we will be the very ones He will gather for His use and for His Heavenly Garden!

Song of Solomon 2:2 (Amplified) also gives us insight. *"like the lily among thorns, so are you my love, among the daughters."* Here, the king (symbolizing Jesus) is complimenting his beloved (believers) and differentiating her from thorns (unbelievers). She's a beautiful lily, but there are thorns around her. It brings to mind Matthew 13:25-30, the parable of the tares and wheat where an enemy had sown tares in the wheat fields. Tares look like wheat but are useless weeds. In verse 30 (Amplified) the owner of the wheat field (who represents God) says, *"Let them grow together until the harvest; and at harvest time I will say to the reapers, Gather the darnel (tares) first and bind it in bundles to be burned, but gather the wheat into my granary."*

Only believers will be gathered into the granary, into the heavenly garden.

Putting all of Song of Solomon 6:2 together we see this amazing picture: The king has gone into his garden **longing** (remember that word "beds" also means longing) and he's **longing** for the sweet fragrance of his planting—**which is us, His treasure!** He desires to feed, to graze (in other words to gather a harvest) but also to take care of his plantings. And he comes as shepherd and as king or lord over the garden, as well as a friend. And he comes specifically to gather **lilies**, which represent those who have been made white by his blood. And like a gleaner, he's come to gather them from among the thorns in order to bring joy, not only to himself, but to them as well. It's a stunning picture of Jesus and His bride, the ones whose hearts belong to Him and are His garden, cultivated for His purpose and pleasure, an exclusive garden in which He has become the center.

And just like the parable of the wheat and tares, it's a picture of the final gathering or gleaning that will take place during the last harvest when Jesus, our Heavenly Gardener, returns.

Gardens produce fruit.

Throughout Scripture, "fruit" refers to produce and the fruit of our body (Deuteronomy 28:4) as well as the fruit our lives and actions produce as seen in the following Scriptures:

Psalm 92:12-14, *"The righteous shall flourish like the palm **tree**: he shall grow like a cedar in Lebanon. Those that be planted in the house of the LORD shall flourish in the courts of our God. They shall bring forth **fruit** in old age: they shall be fat and flourishing."* What a Scripture! Again, man is compared to trees, righteous plantings. Those who have come into the saving knowledge of Jesus will not only produce fruit in old age but will flourish in heaven!

Proverbs 11:30 comes right out and says, *"the fruit of the righteous is a **tree** of life."* And Proverbs 8:19 says, regarding spiritual fruit, *"My **fruit** is better than gold, yea, than fine gold; and my revenue than choice silver."*

Both Ezekiel 7:19 and Isaiah 2:20 tell us that in the last days men will toss their gold and silver into the streets because they are useless. Ezekiel 7:19 says, *"They shall cast their silver in the streets, and their gold shall be removed: their silver and their gold shall not be able to deliver them in the day of the wrath of the LORD."* All that unbelievers strive for, covet, and cling to will be worthless. The only thing that will have lasting value is the fruit our lives produce for God. Our godly fruit will, indeed, be more valuable than gold or silver.

Proverbs 10:16 says that while the labor/fruit of the righteous tends to life, the *"fruit of the wicked* (tends*) to sins."*

Paul, in Romans 6:21, reminded believers that in their former days, before they came to Jesus, they did not produce good fruit. He said, *"What **fruit** had ye then in those things whereof ye are now **ashamed**? For the end of those things is death."* But he added in verse 22, that since coming to Christ they were *"made free from sin, and become servants to God, ye have your **fruit** unto holiness, and the end everlasting life."* What a wonderful change; a change with eternal consequences! After accepting Jesus and allowing the Holy Spirit to produce godly fruit in our lives, we no longer have to be ashamed.

Other Scriptures regarding gardens:

Jeremiah 31:12b, talking about restored Israel, says, *"Their soul shall be as a watered **garden**; and they shall not sorrow any more at all."* That also applies to all restored sinners.

Isaiah 51:3 says that God will make Israel like Eden, the garden of the Lord.

Isaiah 58:11 calls the righteous/the godly, *"a watered **garden**."*

In Numbers 24:6 Balaam sees Israel as *"**gardens** by the riverside."*

Conversely there are gardens NOT of the Lord.

Like the evil one who planted tares in the wheat field, so Satan is also planting his garden. That's why he tries so hard to keep people from coming to the Lord. He blinds their minds. He uses fear and pride. He makes false promises. And he will even elevate to high positions and fame those who worship and commit themselves to him. Many rock stars are examples of this. They worship Satan and even have altar calls during their concerts. Satan has the power and authority to do all this because, for now, he is still the "god of this world." But someday soon that will change when Jesus takes His rightful place on the throne of David.

Isaiah 1:29 tells us the gardens not of the Lord which the people had chosen would bring shame. Isaiah 65:3 and 66:17 talk about these types of gardens where people have sacrificed to idols. Applying it to today, they are the gardens of those who do not seek after God but make other things their god such as success, money, pleasure, etcetera. And Isaiah 1:8 and 1:30 talk about gardens that have no water, and gardens made desolate for abandoning God.

Jesus our Heavenly Gardener:

Jesus is a serious gardener. So is God the Father. In John 15:1-2, Jesus said, *"I AM the true vine, and my Father is the husbandman* (gardener). *Every branch in me that beareth not **fruit** he taketh away: and every branch that beareth **fruit**, he purgeth it, that it may bring forth more **fruit**."* So, those who don't produce the kind of fruit that pleases God, will be "taken away" but those who do will be pruned. Pruning implies cutting away the dead and useless things that retard growth. Expect to be pruned. And expect it to be unpleasant at times.

John the Baptist also made this clear in Matthew 3:9-10. He was speaking to the religious people of the day who thought they had it all together but were far from God. They thought that because they came from the seed of Abraham they were in good standing with God. Just like today, someone might be tempted to think that because he/she was raised in church yet had no relationship with God and lived like the world, was okay, too. *"And think not to say within yourselves, We have Abraham to our father: for I say unto you, that God is able of these stones to raise up children unto Abraham. And now also the ax is laid unto the root of the **trees*** (God was about to judge Israel); ***therefore every tree which bringeth not forth good fruit is hewn down, and cast into the fire.*** *"* Just as God didn't spare judging Israel, so He will not spare judging Gentiles.

And Jesus tells us the only way this pleasing fruit is produced is by abiding in Him. In John 15:4, He said, *"Abide in me, and I in you, As the branch cannot bear **fruit** of itself, except it abide in the vine: no more can ye, except ye abide in me."* It is evident that we, in and of ourselves, are incapable of producing the kind of fruit pleasing to God. We must be connected to Jesus, the Vine, to do it.

23

Romans 7:4-5 expounds on this. *"Wherefore, my brethren, ye also are become dead to the law by the body of Christ; that ye should be married to another, even to him who is raised from the dead, that we should bring forth **fruit unto God**. For when we were in the flesh, the motions of sins, which were by the law, did work in our members to bring forth **fruit unto death**."*

So, how does Jesus produce the fruit He's looking for in us? It's only through the empowerment of the Holy Spirit. Galatians 5:22-23 talks about this fruit and lists them: *"But the **fruit** of the Spirit is love, joy, peace, longsuffering, gentleness, goodness, faith, Meekness, temperance: against such there is no law."*

Then Paul goes on in verses 24-25 to tell us that we are dead to the flesh and alive in the Holy Spirit and we need to walk in His ways. That's the formula for success: accepting Jesus, dying to self, allowing the Holy Spirit to take control and change us. *"And they that are Christ's have crucified the flesh with the affections and lusts. If we live in the Spirit, let us also walk in the Spirit* (in His ways and in His fruit).*"*

It's the Holy Spirit Who imparts this pleasing fruit in us, and if we allow Him to lead and change us, they will become evident in our lives.

And Ephesians 5:9 says, *"For the **fruit** of the Spirit is in all goodness and righteousness and truth."*

Paul, in Philippians 4:17, was also concerned about godly fruit and told the Philippian church that he did not desire a gift, *"but I desire **fruit** that may abound to your account."*

Pleasing fruit of the believer will translate to rewards or crowns during the Bema Judgment. Unpleasing fruit of unbelievers will be judged at the White Throne Judgment. For more on these judgments see my book, *Encountering Jesus Throughout the Bible.*

Since our hearts are God's garden, we need to be careful what we allow into them. We need to protect them from fear, unforgiveness, envy, and the like. We need to keep them pure for the Lord.

Since Jeremiah 17:9 tells us that, *"The heart is deceitful above all things and desperately wicked: who can know it?"* we must understand that even with all our care, we still won't fully know our own heart. Only God really knows it. The best we can do is listen to the words coming out of our mouths, because Jesus said in Matthew 12:34, *"out of the abundance of the heart the mouth speaketh."*

So, our words will give us clues as to what is in our heart. If we are complaining, gossiping, fault-finding, that's a sure indication that it's time for our Gardener, Jesus, to pull some weeds and replace them with the fruit of the Spirit. If we allow Him to do it, we will have a garden that our precious Lord will find pleasing and enjoyable. May it be so!

The Heavenly Garden

This is the **Final Garden.** Just as God in Genesis 2:8 planted a garden in Eden, so Jesus is planting a garden in heaven. And it's the final garden. We are His plantings to be eventually taken up to heaven for His enjoyment and ours, a planting exclusively His. And as a planting in God's garden, we will flourish, be watered, and protected by God Himself.

In Revelation 22:1-2 (Amplified), which speaks of a new heaven, a new earth and a new Jerusalem, an angel showed John *"the river whose waters give life, sparkling like crystal, flowing out from the throne of God and of the Lamb through the middle of the broadway of the city, also, on either side of the river was the tree of life with its twelve varieties of fruit, yielding each month its fresh crop, and the leaves of the tree were for the healing and restoration of the nations."*

John saw the place containing the tree of life. It's the place where we will be God's delight and He will be ours. Remember how Balaam saw Israel as "gardens by the riverside." As believers this also applies to us. It is in this riverside garden that believers, both Jew and Gentile, will be planted one day. A place where we will partake of the tree of life and live for all eternity with our King, Saviour and Friend.

So, when we go through times of trials and testing, we need to remember what Jesus, the Heavenly Gardener, is trying to do. He's trying to make something beautiful out of us, a garden He can enjoy now, as well as a future planting in His very own heavenly garden.

*"Now no chastening for the present seemeth to be joyous, but grievous: nevertheless afterward it yieldeth the peaceable **fruit** of righteousness unto them which are exercised thereby."* Hebrews 12:11

Section Two

Valleys of Man

There are over fifty named valleys in the Bible, as well as several unnamed ones that are simply called "the rough valley" or "fat valley" or "the valley" etcetera, but all with a story to tell and a lesson to impart. This section will cover only those that seem most relevant. And as we go through them, we need to remember they are but opportunities for God to show Himself mighty.

In Old Testament times, the term "valley" often carried a negative connotation in the minds of the Israelites. Primarily mountain dwellers, the Israelites were surrounded by valleys inhabited by their foes. These valleys or lowlands usually fell into two categories: a plain or wide expanse of land and a gorge formed by streams that had carved out large masses of limestone and sand. These gorges were usually harsh and difficult to maneuver. Ironically, many of Israel's battles were fought in both these areas. Thus, valleys are often associated with trials and testing.

The Bible is full of typology and foreshadowing, gems waiting to be excavated. Valleys are one such example. What makes them so interesting is that much of man's earthly journey appears to be a cycle of going from high to low points in often seemingly random fashion. Because of that, these Biblical valleys have great lessons to impart, and not all are negative, as we shall see.

But when we find ourselves in the negative ones, there is great encouragement to be had. Isaiah 40:3-5 is a wonderful Messianic promise. *"The **voice** of him that crieth in the wilderness, Prepare ye the way of the LORD, make straight in the desert a highway for our God. **Every valley shall be exalted**, and every mountain and hill shall be made low: and the crooked shall be made straight, and the rough places plain: And the glory of the LORD shall be revealed, and all flesh shall see it together: for the mouth of the LORD hath spoken it."*

Of course, the "voice" is that of John the Baptist who proclaimed Jesus was the Messiah and Lamb of God. And it is because Jesus came and died for us that we have a wonderful future in heaven. But we don't have to wait. Jesus can do wonderful things in the "here and now." If we let Him, He can take those low points in our lives, those valleys, and transform them into something good. That's His promise to us. We don't have to allow our valleys to defeat us or make us afraid.

Then in 1 Kings 20:28 there's this: *"And there came a man of God, and spake unto the king of Israel, and said, Thus saith the LORD, Because the Syrians have said, The LORD is God of the hills,* **but he is not God of the valleys,** *therefore will I deliver all this great multitude into thine hand, and ye shall know that I am the LORD."*

The king of Syria, Ben-hadad, along with thirty-two other kings, came against Samaria with an overwhelming army, yet they were defeated. The spiritual implication is this: when Satan comes against us with overwhelming force, presenting us with an enormous problem, believe that God will be there and help us handle it because God isn't just God of the good

times. He's also there with us in our valleys, and
He is more than able to give us victory.

Valley of Shinar

The first valley mentioned in the Bible is the Valley of Shinar (Genesis 11:2). It's located in southern Mesopotamia between the Euphrates and Tigris rivers. First mentions are generally significant. And that word "valley" here is no exception. Some translations call this valley, a plain. In Hebrew, it's the word *biqah* and means, "a wide level valley between mountains." But it also means, "to rend, rip, or make a breach."

By Genesis 11:2, a lot had happened. Adam and Eve had been tossed out of the Garden of Eden and their descendants had fallen prey to sin. Because things got so bad, God flooded the earth, destroying everyone and everything in it except eight people—Noah and his family. We come upon the Valley of Shinar after the flood story. It is where the current inhabitants of the world had chosen to dwell, contrary to God's command to replenish and repopulate the whole earth, not just this section of it.

Genesis 11:1-2 says, *"And the whole earth was of one language and of one speech. And it came to pass, as they* (the descendants of Noah) *journeyed from the east, that they found **a plain in the land of Shinar***; *and they dwelt there."*

You would think that after the expulsion from the garden and the destruction of civilization by a flood, that man would be more mindful of God; that they would tread lightly and try to do what pleased Him. But no. The Valley of Shinar is the valley of rebellion with the tyrant, Nimrod, at its head. It was the center of idolatry and the occult, birthing Mystery Babylon, the Mother of Harlots, the fountainhead of all counterfeit religions. It is here that the people were building the Tower of Babel to *"reach unto heaven"* and *"make a name"* for themselves.

Genesis 11:3-4, *"And they said one to another, Go to, let us make brick and burn them thoroughly. And they had brick for stone, and **slime** had they for morter. And they said, Go to, let us build us a city and a tower, **whose top may reach unto heaven**; and let us make us a name, lest we be scattered abroad upon the face of the whole earth."*

34

On a corporate level, these people were setting up a one-world government to replace God. On an individual level they were magnifying "self". But notice, they used slime for mortar. It was the same slime or pitch that Noah used to waterproof the ark. This showed their utter contempt for God. By waterproofing the tower, the people were telling God that if He decided to flood the earth again, they would be ready. Their tower would be watertight and high enough (*"whose top may reach unto heaven"*) to withstand His efforts.

Nimrod and the Tower of Babel, and his role in a future one world government and one world religion is covered in my book, *The Coming Deception*, and is too long to recap here. But suffice it to say, this was no minor rebellion. It had far reaching consequences, consequences which remain even to this day.

Rejecting God or rebelling against Him will always bring us to the Valley of Shinar, the kind of valley that will "rend, rip, or make a breach" in our relationship with God and each other. I can't think of a sadder place to be.

And how did God react to Nimrod's efforts? First, He confounded their language, then He scattered them. On one level it was an act of mercy. His concern was evident when He said, *"now nothing will be restrained from them which they have imagined to do,"* (Genesis 11:6b). God foresaw that if they were allowed to continue with their wickedness it would necessitate judgment on His part. But on another level, it was deeply tragic since people were now confused, isolated, aimless, and limited in their ability to communicate; all mirroring the isolation, confusion, and aimlessness of life without God. And what a hopeless life that is, when self occupies the position that belongs to Him! Oh, may we never find ourselves in the Valley of Shinar!

Instead of becoming their own god and making a name for themselves, what Nimrod and his people accomplished was to alienate themselves from the one true God who loved them and had their best interest at heart, and to alienate themselves from one another. Tragically, but not surprising, this led to the next valley—the Valley of Siddim—the scene of the very first war described in the Bible.

Valley of Siddim

Many years had passed since the Tower of Babel. People had spread in all directions. But a good portion, after leaving the valley of rebellion (Shinar), found themselves in the Valley of Siddim. Also called the Valley of Salt, it contained salt flats and bitumen pits. While salt is a positive thing in that it's a preservative against decay and contamination, it also has a negative connotation. It can indicate barrenness since that was the substance scattered over a city devoted to God for destruction, thus making that land barren and unable to produce. It was also used by Israel's enemies to destroy their land and make it desolate.

In this same way, Satan will "salt" our lives with temptation and adversity in order to make it a wasteland. While we are here on earth, his goal is to "steal, kill, and destroy" (John 10:10) hoping we never come to Jesus, thus causing us, after we die, to spend eternity in hell and ensure our final destruction there.

Returning to the Valley of Siddim: it was the valley of destruction and strife, where the first recorded war in Scripture took place. I suppose that's to be expected. If we don't have peace with God, can we have peace with our fellow man? Doubtful.

This area was now controlled by nine kings with the head king being Chedorlaomer. For twelve years the other kings served Chedorlaomer (Genesis 14). Finally, in the thirteenth year, five of the kings rebelled, including the King of Sodom and the King of Gomorrah, and within a year, Chedorlaomer marched against them with his army and the army of his three allies. So, it was four kings against five.

The four kings were able to vanquish the others and took them as spoils of war along with their goods, livestock, children, and wives. Among those taken was Lot, Abraham's nephew, who had, some time before, left Abraham to live in Sodom.

During this time, Abraham dwelt safely by the mountain of Mamre. God had already called him to separate himself from the world, to leave the Ur of the Chaldees, a place of gross idolatry, and go to a land that He would show him. And though it would be Abraham's descendants who would eventually enter the Promised Land and not Abraham himself, he would, all his life, live as a "stranger and pilgrim on the earth" (Hebrews 11:13), yearning for *"a city which hath foundations, whose builder and maker is God,"* (Hebrews 11:10). That city, of course, is heaven itself, which is symbolized by the Promised Land. In addition, God had told Abraham He would make him a great nation. And He did just that. Abraham became the patriarch of the twelve tribes of Israel, the very chosen people of God.

This is also a wonderful picture of the believer. Like Abraham, we, too, are "strangers and pilgrims" called by God to be separated from the world; to refrain from its sin and strife. 1 John 5:19 says *"the whole world lieth in wickedness."* And Romans 12:2a cautions us to, *"be not conformed to this world."* While 1 John 2:15 admonishes us to, *"love not the world neither the things that are in the world. If any man love the world, the love of the Father is not in him."* James 4:4 goes even further and tells us that to be friends with the world is to be an enemy of God.

And like Abraham, we should always keep in mind that this world in not our real home. Heaven is. And someday we will go there to live with God forever. What a happy thought!

But like Abraham, who, when he heard about Lot's capture, was forced to take up arms and rescue him, sometimes we, too, are pulled into the war and conflict around us, and are called into battle. This, of course, refers to a spiritual battle. There will always be someone who causes strife in our world, someone who wants to rule, to control, to subjugate. In the larger sense we think of people like Hitler or Bin Laden, but on a smaller scale it could be that difficult boss or abusive spouse or impossible neighbor or co-worker. And when we encounter them, we are called to be uncompromising in our faith while showing them the love of Jesus, as well as interceding for them in prayer.

So, because of others, there will be times when we must leave our mountainside of peace for the valley of strife, pulled there by a war or conflict not of our making. And like Abraham and his men who prevailed and rescued Lot and the other captives, so we, too, if we faithfully follow God's leading, will prevail in our struggles and battles.

The Valley of Salt (Siddim) is mentioned again in 2 Samuel 8:13 where King David wars against the Syrians (named "Syrians" in the King James version) and achieves a great victory thus making a name for himself and increasing his fame. However, the Amplified version of 2 Samuel 8:13 doesn't call these foes, "Syrians" but "Edomites." So does the Septuagint, the Scriptures read during Old Testament times and the ones Jesus quoted. It calls them "Idumea," which means, "red" (a name for Esau) or "Edom" confirming they were Edomites. Years later, according to 2 Kings 14:7, Judah's godly king Amaziah also had a great victory over the Edomites in the Valley of Salt.

Why is this important? The Edomites were descendants of Jacob's brother, Esau. They harbored an ancient hated for Israel (Jacob) and became one of their primary enemies. They were known for their violence, pride, unrighteousness, and being haters of God. Their name became synonymous with evil. Herod the Great and his clan were Edomites. They were descendants of Esau not Jacob, which is why many Jews disliked them and found it difficult to accept them as rightful rulers over Israel.

And Edomites—symbolic of violence, pride, unrighteousness, hatred of God and godliness—are the very enemies we must face in the Valley of Siddim or valley of strife. They are the very "salt" Satan uses to try to destroy our lives. But Romans 8:37 tells us that *"we are more than conquerors through him* (Christ Jesus) *that loved us."* How wonderful to know that the Holy Spirit will enable us to overpower these enemies and when we do, we, too, like David, will gain a reputation for how we, in godliness, walk through strife; how we, in the midst of trials and tribulations, maintain our peace, joy, and love of the Lord. And it's all due to HIM!

Valley of Shaveh

Since valleys often symbolize low points in our lives, I was surprised to find Abraham in the Valley of Shaveh right after his victory over King Chedorlaomer, (Genesis 14:17-20). Why was he there and not back on the mountainside? Only after much thought did it seem reasonable to see Abraham in another low point. God had given him a great victory, but the victory came with a price. The Bible calls what happened in the last valley, the Valley of Siddim, a "slaughter". Abraham had been at war. He had blood on his hands. He had killed many. And he had made enemies. Would their sons or relatives seek revenge? These things had to weigh heavily on his mind and rob him of his peace.

But here's the good part. Genesis 14:18-20 tells us that while Abraham lingered in this low point, Melchizedek, priest of the most high God and King of Salem, came to him. *"And Melchizedek king of Salem brought forth bread and wine: and he was the priest of the most high God. And he blessed him* (Abraham), *and said, Blessed be Abram of the most high God, possessor of heaven and earth: And blessed be the most high God, which hath delivered thine enemies into thy hand. And he* (Abraham) *gave him tithes of all."*

Who was this Melchizedek, this King of Salem? His name gives us a clue. Salem means peace; thus, He is the King of Peace. He also comes bearing bread and wine, and blessed Abraham. And he is priest of the most high God. Hebrews 7:1-3, speaking of Jesus, says, *"For this Melchisedec, king of Salem, priest of the most high God, who met Abraham returning from the slaughter of the kings, and blessed him; To whom also Abraham gave a tenth part of all; first being by interpretation King of righteousness, and after that also King of Salem, which is King of peace; Without father, without mother, without descent, having neither beginning of days, for end of life; but made like unto the Son of God; abideth a priest continually."* Hebrews 5:6, also tells us this about Jesus: *"Thou are a priest forever after the order of Melchisedec."*

There is only One Who fills this bill. By calling him King of Righteousness and telling us he had no parents or beginning nor end of days, and saying he was "like unto the Son of God," these Scriptures indicate Melchizedek was the pre-incarnate Jesus, the ever existing One who appears many times in the Old Testament.

Melchizedek blessed Abraham and reminded him of who he belonged to. Genesis 14:19, *"blessed be Abram of the most high God, possessor of heaven and earth."* And this helped Abraham remember the faithfulness and awesomeness of God, while assuring him that God was still with him, thus restoring his peace.

It's interesting to note that while Shaveh means a plain, its prime root means, "to level, equalize, to adjust, compose, counterbalance." That's just what Abraham needed, an adjustment, something to counterbalance what he had just gone through and bring composure and calm in order to rid him of his fears. And praise God, that's just what Jesus did for Abraham as Melchizedek.

What does it say to us? After we have been in the Valley of Siddim, a valley of conflict and strife, and the conflict is over, it may be difficult to regain our peace. So many unpleasant things happen during a conflict. Sometimes we're called to confront someone, to speak the truth in love. People are wounded. Relationships may be destroyed. And this could leave us trapped in a valley of remorse or despondency or fear of the unknown. But praise God, Jesus is willing and able to meet us just like He did Abraham and do the same for us and restore our peace. And if we commune with Him (symbolized by the bread and wine brought by Melchizedek), if we spend time in fellowship with Him, He will restore us to a place of peace, and bless us going forward. What a gracious God we serve!

Valley of Gerar

Beware of this valley. It's dangerous. The name Gerar, itself, means, "to drag off roughly." What happened here? In Genesis 26:12-22, Isaac, Abraham's son, has been mightily blessed by God and has become *"very great."* But a famine forced him to move near the Philistines in King Abimelech's territory. Because Isaac was so blessed, the Philistines were envious, and their envy drove them to stop up Isaac's wells. Water is vital, especially in the Middle East, so this was serious, even life threatening.

Eventually, King Abimelech got involved and, in the interest of peace, asked Isaac to leave, thus Isaac was symbolically "dragged off roughly," to the valley of Gerar and had to relocate his entire household. But even here his troubles didn't end because the new wells his herdsmen dug were contested by the herdsmen of Gerar. After a cycle of digging wells then giving them up to the protesters, Isaac finally dug a well that he could keep.

So, why do I think this is a dangerous valley? Because it's a valley that can easily breed resentment and bitterness. Imagine you are happy, "on top of the world," and living in peaceful union with God, blessed mightily by Him, when suddenly, because of the sins or selfishness or carelessness or malevolence of others you are forced to go to a place you don't want to go; forced to endure hardship, suffering, heartache, humiliation, all because of something someone else did. It could be a spouse who didn't handle the finances wisely and now you are facing bankruptcy, or a spouse who has violated the marriage with an adulterous affair, or a business that has been mismanaged and now you are out of a job, or a rebellious child who has run away or committed a crime, turning your world upside down. It could be any one of a dozen things, but the result is the same. You find yourself where you don't want to be, "dragged" there by someone else. And because you believe it's not your fault, bitterness can take root.

Genesis 26:19 tells us that in the midst of this valley, Isaac's servants found a *"well of springing water* (KJV)." The Amplified calls it a *"well of living (spring) water."* Jesus tells us in John 4:10 that He will give "living water" to whoever asks. It's the only kind of water capable of quenching spiritual thirst. In essence, He is that living water able to satiate and sustain us no matter how "rough" the circumstance become.

Gerar is a tough valley to be sure, but oh, what a deep and marvelous well God has for us there if only we ask! It doesn't have to be a place of bitterness. It can be a place where circumstances make us more open to the Lord, as well as a place of deep refreshing. As usual, the choice is ours.

Valley of Eshcol

Time has moved on. Joseph has saved the Egyptians and his family from starvation. Then for 400 years the Israelites suffered under Egyptian bondage before God, through Moses, delivered them and took them into the desert to forge them into a new nation. Abraham, Isaac, and Jacob all had covenants with God which included the promise of a specific land mass. Now, it was time for their descendants to claim that Promised Land.

Enter the Valley of Eshcol. It is a sample of the Promised Land where a cluster of grapes was so large and heavy that two of the twelve spies Moses sent to scout the land, *"bare it between two upon a staff"* (Numbers 13:23). A land of plenty, it was also a land of giants and walled cities. And here in was the rub. In order for the Hebrews to obtain the territory God had promised them, the territory of incredible prosperity and plenty, they had to face and overcome obstacles.

Did they meet the challenge? Only two of the spies returned with a good report, proclaiming that they were well able to take the land. The other ten painted such a dark and foreboding picture that the Israelites became too frightened to go.

Numbers 13:31-33, *"But the men that went up with him* (Caleb who had just given a good report of the Promised Land) *said, We be not able to go up against the people; for they are stronger than we. And they brought up an evil report of the land which they had searched unto the children of Israel, saying, The land, through which we have gone to search it, is a land that eateth up the inhabitants thereof; and all the people that we saw in it are men of a great stature. And there we saw the giants, the sons of Anak, which come of the giants: and we were in our own sight as* **grasshoppers***, and so we were in their sight."*

Notice, they saw themselves as grasshoppers! As little insignificant nothings. Yes, they were not trained soldiers and were smaller in stature than their opponents, but they forgot they had a mighty God. In addition, they had seen enough of God's faithfulness and power to understand that because God had already told them this land was theirs, He would honor His Word and see it fulfilled.

Lacking the faith to take what God had given them, the Israelites wandered the wilderness for forty years, one year for each day the twelve men had originally spied out the Promised Land. Now, all the men of that generation, except Caleb and Joshua, had died. So, it fell to the next generation to finally claim their inheritance (Numbers 32:9-13). What a tragic story!

Those who have been in the Valley of Eshcol know there is always a choice to be made here. Rich and ripe with the promises of God, it also comes with obstacles, with giants and high walls that need overcoming. Ask any person in a vibrant ministry, a ministry that is touching hearts for God and furthering His kingdom, and I guarantee he/she will tell you that their ministry has been brought about at great cost. But the same can be said of our personal lives. The promises God makes us often seem to take forever to materialize, and there seems to be one wall after another to be scaled, one giant after another that hinders our progress. That wayward child God has promised to deliver from drugs seems to be only getting worse; instead of that healing God promised we seem to get sicker; and rather than God's promised provision, our finances continue sinking deeper into the red. The list goes on.

In this valley, much is at stake. Like the Hebrews, we can throw up our hands and say the giants are too big, the walls too high. We can say that victory is impossible, and God's promises will never come to pass. Or, we can be like Caleb and Joshua, who, because of their trust in God, were the only two spies out of the original twelve permitted to enter the Promised Land along with the new generation. The fact is, it doesn't matter if we are weak or as small as grasshoppers compared to our large problems, we serve a BIG God Who is more than able to make us victorious.

But we must understand that God's ways are higher than ours and He doesn't measure time the way we do. But if we stay the course, no matter how long it takes, His promises will come to pass. How do I know? Because God doesn't lie. Because God is able to do whatever He has promised. And because God never fails. He can do the impossible.

However, once we have decided to enter the Valley of Eschol and face all the obstacles, there is still one hazard left. Galatians 6:9 says, *"Let us not be **weary** in well doing; for in due season we **shall** reap, if we faint not."* Becoming weary is a real and present danger. It's actually one of the biggest dangers in this valley. Because the fight can be long and hard, it's easy to become weary and give up before we see victory. When we are tempted to do so, we must strengthen ourselves in Jesus Who tells us that His strength is made perfect in weakness, (2 Corinthians 12:9). Oh, how wonderful He is!

Valleys of Zared, Bamoth, and Bashan

The Israelites had blown their chance. They had been delivered from the slave pits of Egypt by the mighty hand of God but proved cowardly in the Valley of Eschol. So, instead of taking just a few months to enter their Promised Land, they now seemed to be wandering aimlessly in the dessert. And the next three valleys are symbolic of that journey. In many ways, they also reflect the journey believers often take after being delivered from the slave pits of the world. Let's see what lessons they provide.

The wanderings of the Israelites often appeared pointless and haphazard, but God was doing something amazing. He was forging a nation, a peculiar people unto Himself, just as He does with believers. He takes us on a journey, sometimes seemingly pointless and haphazard, but each step is calculated to bring us closer to fulfilling the plan He has for our lives and to fashion us into the person He wants us to be. And yes, that often means hardship and adversity.

Prior to arriving at the **Valley of Zared**, the Israelites had done their share of grumbling against God. Then they had to endure the plague of snakes when God finally got tired of it. And only after Moses, on God's orders, had erected a bronze serpent on a pole, did they get a remedy. From there they had gone to Oboth and Ijeabarim, rough and dry terrains, before arriving at the Valley of Zared also called Zered, a lush place containing a stream. Numbers 21:12 says that the Israelites, *"pitched in the **Valley of Zared.**"*

Zared means, "exuberant in growth." Because of the water supply it was full of vegetation. The snakes, the dry, barren desert, the endless hiking, all were God's means of strengthening His people, of making them "exuberant in growth." Nothing makes one grow or mature faster than hardship. God was working in them the very character needed to procure their Promised Land.

How well that reflects the life of a new Christian. After coming to the Lord, we often first experience a heady sense of freedom much like the Israelites must have felt after their release from Egyptian bondage. But after a while, it becomes evident that life hasn't changed much. The old life, the old habits and ways of thinking are still very evident. But how could that be? Our desire to change is strong. So is the desire to get closer to God, to live a godly life and be pleasing to Him. Instead, it seems we are still rooted in the old barren soil and look little like that spiritual powerhouse the Bible talks about.

And why does it feel like we are on an aimless hike? Tramping around in a dry desert where nothing seems to grow? What was God doing? And then comes the stream in the valley that reveals, yes, there is growth, there is shrubbery in the baren landscape, and even some evidence of fruit popping out, the fruit of the Holy Spirit. Oh, how wonderful! And how it delights and refreshes because we suddenly realize we are not the same. We **have** changed. And this watered valley is enough to fortify us for the journey ahead, when once again we will encounter the dry and rutted desert roads. But now we approach it with renewed vigor because we know that it is here, in these harsh places, where God will change us.

It's interesting to note that thirty-eight years after the Israelites left Kadesh-barne-a they again passed through the Valley of Zared (Zered). *"Now rise up, said I (God), and get you over the brook **Zered**. And we went over the brook **Zered**. And the space in which we came from Kadesh-barne-a, until we were come over the brook **Zered**, was thirty and eight years; until all the generation of the men of war were wasted out (died) from among the host, as the LORD sware unto them,"* Deuteronomy 2:13-14. Two years had elapsed prior to them arriving at Kadesh-barnea then leaving it for this trip to the Valley of Zared, which ended their forty years of wandering. They had evidenced "exuberant growth" and were getting ready to appropriate their inheritance.

Just as it took Israel forty years to finally enter the Promised Land, so it takes believers time to grow in the Lord, to understand His ways, to be equipped and able to appropriate His promises for their lives and able to do spiritual warfare when claiming their inheritance. Even so, it is a journey that never ends as long as we live on planet earth. And though we are being changed from "glory to glory" there will always be more to learn, more ways in which to grow. Praise God, He is so patient with us!

From their earlier journey to the Valley of Zared in Numbers 21:12, it wasn't long after that the Israelites traveled to the **Valley of Bamoth**. A town in Moab surrounded by high cliffs, its plain was more gorge than valley. The name "Bamoth" means," "heights, heights of Baal or high places of Baal." And that word "valley" here is *gay* and means, "exaltation, arrogance." It was a place of idol worship, specifically of Baal; a place where people exalted themselves and their idols above the God of Abraham, Isaac, Jacob. Later, it would be from these mountains overlooking the Valley of Bamoth that King Balak would bring the prophet Balaam to speak a curse over Israel (Joshua 13:17) again displaying arrogance and pride before God.

It's an important valley, one we must all walk through. And there will come a time when God takes us there in order to reveal those idols in our lives, those things or people we have exalted and placed above Him. We need to understand that God considers idolatry to be adultery. Israel is God's bride, and the Church is Jesus' bride, and idolatry is akin to being a faithless wife in the eyes of God.

And there's a play on words here. Remember Bamoth means "high places of Baal." Baal was a major Canaanite deity while ba 'al is the Hebrew word for husband. And God called Himself Israel's husband. *"For thy Maker is thine husband* (ba'al) *the LORD of hosts is his name,"* Isaiah 54:5. It is in the Valley of Bamoth where God exposes false baals in order to become the true ba 'al in our lives.

The **Valley of Bashan** is another important valley. Before the Israelites crossed the Jordon to begin their campaign of claiming the land, they passed through Bashan. It's a broad, fertile plateau on the east side of upper Jordan. Once inhabited by the Rephaim or giants, now the only giant left in that area was King Og. He was massive, needing a 13 ½ foot bed. Deuteronomy 3:11 says, *"For only Og king of Bashan remained of the giants; behold his bedstead was a bedstead of iron; is it not in Rabbath of the children of Ammon? Nine cubits was the length thereof, and four cubits the breadth of it, after the cubit of a man* (18 inches)."

Now, this giant and his army stood between them and entrance to their Promised Land. It was the presence of giants that dissuaded the Israelites 40 years before from entering the land. All those men who hadn't trusted the Lord had died. Now, this new generation was here to claim their inheritance, but a giant stood in the way. One giant, one more test. Would this new generation fail, too? In Deuteronomy 3:2 God encouraged Moses to challenge Og. *"And the LORD said unto me, Fear him not: for I will deliver him, and all his people, and his land, into thy hand; and thou shalt do unto him as thou didst unto Sihon king of the Amorites, which dwelt at Heshbon."*

Here, God was giving them a chance to overcome the mistakes of the past and telling them "I've got this, don't be afraid." So, what happened in the Valley of Bashan? *"the LORD our God delivered into our hands Og also, the king of Bashan, and all his people: and we smote him **until none was left to him remaining**."* It was a total victory. The Israelites ended up destroying 60 cities of Bashan, and its territory was given to the half tribe of Manasseh.

Like the new generation of Israelites, we are a new creature in Christ Jesus. He makes all things new. 2 Corinthians 5:17, *"Therefore if any man be in Christ, he is a new creature: old things are passed away; behold all things are become new."*

And we have experienced the Valley of Zared and have grown in our faith. Now, we are ready to appropriate our destiny except there's a problem. A giant stands in the way—the giant of our past. It's a giant that can paralyze us. It's a giant Satan often uses, for he loves bringing up our past—all those mistakes—and throwing them in our face. He will use them to tell us we don't qualify for anything meaningful, that God can't use us. And if that past has been especially rough, say involving drugs or a crime of some kind, he will try to convince us that this is as far as we can hope to go. That maybe we might have gotten salvation, but that's all we can expect, so forget about a ministry or active Christian life. It's too late. There's too much muddy water under the bridge. We will never be more than a second-class citizen in God's kingdom. And when that happens, don't believe him!

Paul tells us in Philippians 3:13-14, to forget the past in order to *"press toward the mark for the prize of the high calling of God in Christ Jesus."* We must forget the past in order to press into our present and future. Dwelling in the past can make one "stuck" and unable to move forward into their God-given destiny.

As new creatures, the Valley of Bashan gives us an opportunity to put our past behind us. Though we can't change the mistakes we've made or the mistakes our parents have made, and though there may be lingering consequences from those mistakes, we can't let them hinder us. We can't allow them to stand in the way of the many promises God has for us.

And to our amazement, we may even find that God will use those mistakes for His purpose and glory. He is, after all, the God of the impossible! Look at Joyce Meyer. Surviving mental, physical, and sexual abuse at the hands of her father, she has turned this sad past into a vibrant ministry where she is relatable and can speak into hurting hearts. Others who have had abortions are able to counsel those planning one. And remember Chuck Colson? Special Counsel to President Nixon, he was found guilty of obstructing justice during the Watergate scandal and served seven months in federal prison. While incarcerated, he came to the Lord, then established Prison Fellowship, an impactful ministry that continues after his death and is active in all 50 states.

The list is endless, showing the mercy, love, and ability of God to use our weakness and checkered past for His kingdom. Praise His wonderful name!

Valley of Achor

This is not a valley you want to visit. Something terrible happened here. The Israelites had just experienced a stunning victory. God had collapsed the walls of Jericho so their army could breach the city and destroy it. And in Joshua 6:17, He had declared Jericho was cursed and therefore must be destroyed completely. *"And the city shall be **accursed**, even it, and all that are therein, to the LORD: only **Rahab** the harlot shall live, she and all that are with her in the house, because she hid the messengers that we sent."* When something was declared "accursed" by God nothing was to be left standing, not the people, animals, or buildings. In addition, Jericho was a type of "first fruits" to be offered to God as they began their conquest of the Promised Land.

Just a side note regarding Rahab. Her story illustrates the great love and mercy of God. Rahab was a prostitute and idol worshipper.

Talk about a checkered past! Nevertheless, because she had faith that God would destroy Jericho, she helped the two Hebrew spies who were sent to check out the city. She hid them, then instructed them in how they could avoid Jericho's search party. But in return, she made them promise that when the time came, they would spare her and her family. And she was indeed spared. Not only that, but she married Salmon, a man from the tribe of Judah and together they had Boaz. From the line of Boaz came King David and from the line of King David came Jesus. So, included in Jesus' blood line were not only Gentiles, but a prostitute! God indeed is no respecter of persons. He loves us all and desires all to come into the saving knowledge of Him. May it be so!

Returning to Joshua: Unbeknownst to Joshua, God's command was violated and not everything was destroyed in Jericho. So, when Joshua sent three thousand of his soldiers to besiege Ai, a city with fewer men, he thought victory was assured. What a surprise when Ai's smaller contingency rousted Israel's larger army, sending them packing and even killing thirty-six. How could that be? Especially after their spectacular victory at Jericho, a much larger and more dangerous city? Something was wrong.

After Joshua tore his clothes in grief and shame, then prostrated himself before the Ark of the Covenant, God gave him the answer. *"Israel hath sinned, and they have also transgressed my covenant which I commanded them:* **for they have even taken of the accursed thing***, and have also stolen, and dissemble also, and they have put it even among their own stuff. Therefore the children of Israel could not stand before their enemies, but turned their backs before their enemies* (ran away) *because they were* **accursed***: neither will I be with you any more, except ye destroy the* **accursed** *from among you,"* Joshua 7:11-12.

So, that was it. Someone had kept spoils from Jericho and in doing so polluted the entire camp of Israel. And God would have none of it. He would not protect them or go before them in battle until this sin was expunged.

Joshua well understood the ramifications of what had happened. Word would get out how Israel's larger army was cowed and made to run away by Ai's smaller one. Now, the pagan inhabitants of the Promised Land would have no fear of Israel. Unless God intervened, their campaign was lost before it barely got off the ground.

69

Knowing all this, Joshua was careful to follow God's ensuing instructions in Joshua 7:13: *"Up, sanctify the people, and say, Sanctify yourselves against to morrow: for thus saith the LORD God of Israel, There is an* **accursed** *thing in the midst of thee, O Israel: thou canst not stand before thine enemies, until ye take away the* **accursed** *things from among you."* Though God's anger was kindled, He would be merciful. He, Himself, would expose the offending party.

This is what they did next: the following morning all the tribes assembled, then God called out the tribe of Judah. From them, He called out the families, then the households, then the men of each household until only Achan was left. After being questioned by Joshua, Achan confessed. *"When I saw among the spoils a goodly Babylonish garment, and two hundred shekels of silver, and a wedge of gold of fifty shekels weight, then I coveted them, and took them; and behold, they are hid in the earth in the midst of my tent, and the silver under it,"* Joshua 7:21.

The sin was exposed. Achan's covetousness and greed had caused Israel to lose the battle at Ai. But more importantly, they had caused Israel to lose the favor of God.

One must understand that Jericho, like other cities in the Promised Land, was a place of gross idolatry. Demons can inhabit idols as well as people, and it is not a stretch to say this was a place and people possessed by demons. Also, it was a Canaanite custom to sacrifice babies and place their bones in the foundation or walls of homes in dedication to their gods. Therefore, it is not unreasonable to believe that those in Jericho, a Canaanite city, practiced this as well. In addition, Jericho was a place of temple prostitutes and gross sexual sins, which included bestiality. In the occult, ritual sex is often used to transmit demons from person to person. Thus, all Jericho was to be dedicated to God for destruction.

Jericho was considered so evil that Joshua even cursed it in Joshua 6:26, *"And Joshua adjured them at that time, saying, Cursed be the man before the Lord, that riseth up and buildeth this city Jericho: he shall lay the foundation thereof in his firstborn, and in his youngest son shall he set up the gates of it."* This curse was fulfilled years later. The oldest son of Hiel the Bethelite died when Hiel laid Jericho's foundation. Then Hiel's youngest son died when he hung the gates.

God has a reason for everything He does. Even when our minds can't grasp it or we think God's actions severe, we need to understand that there are things happening in the spiritual realm that is beyond our knowing. But God knows what He is doing. And when we get to heaven, we will have a better understanding of what those reasons were. For more about why cities like Jericho were so accursed, see my book *The Coming Deception*.

Because of what happened at Ai, there was no way Joshua could let Achan's sin stand. Israel's entire future rested on making it right. And the remedy? Enter the Valley of Achor. *"And Joshua, and all Israel with him, took Achan the son of Zerah, and the silver, and the garment, and the wedge of gold, and his sons, and his daughters, and his oxen, and his asses, and his sheep, and his tent, and all that he had: and they brought them unto the **valley of Achor**. And Joshua said, Why hast thou troubled us? The LORD shall trouble thee this day. And all Israel stoned him with stones, and burned them with fire, after they had stoned them with stones,"* Joshua 7:24-25.

What a valley! Achor means, "trouble." *The Theological Wordbook of the Old Testament* goes further, and referring to the meaning of Achor, talks about how a person's action can bring trouble on not only himself but others and even a nation, necessitating either man's or God's judgment.

But how does that apply to us? Like the Israelites, as believers we are trying to possess our Promised Land. Then some "accursed" thing hinders our progress and we can't go any further. God won't allow it. He loves us too much because possessing the accursed thing makes us accursed. In addition, holding on to accursed things can bring trouble not only to us but to others, our family, our friends, even our neighborhoods. So, God will act. 1 Peter 4:17 tells us that judgment begins at the house of the Lord.

But just what are these "accursed" things? Those who have come out of the occult will instantly recognize them. They are the paraphernalia of witchcraft, those objects or books they used in their former life. If any remain, they can be the future source of demonic contact. What about ill-gotten gain? Things stolen from others or during a crime are also accursed. So are illicit drugs, for they are gateways to the demonic realm. So are busts of idols, which are so popular in home décor today. Accursed things can also include certain movies or types of music. But rest assured, God will advise us of what is offensive to Him and if we are obedient and relinquish them, there will be no need to travel to the Valley of Achor and feel God's burning displeasure.

This is a necessary step because believers are admonished to be separated. 2 Corinthians 6:16-17 says, *"And what agreement hath the temple of God with idols? For ye are the temple of the living God; as God hath said, I will dwell in them, and walk in them; and I will be their God, and they shall be my people. Wherefore come out from among them, and be ye separate, saith the Lord, and touch not the unclean thing; and I will receive you."*

But here's the good news. Even if we are taken to the Valley of Achor because we failed to rid ourselves of some accursed thing, but then are finally obedient and destroy it, and follow God with all heart, then God can turn the burning ash pile of Achor to a place of plush growth as in Isaiah 65:10; and a door of hope as in Hosea 2:15, *"And I (God) will give her* (referring to Israel when she turns to Him but also includes obedient believers in Jesus) *her vineyards from thence, and the **valley of Achor for a door of hope**: and she shall sing there, as in the days of her youth,* *and as in the day when she came up out of the land of Egypt."*

So, Achor, instead of being a valley of judgment and destruction, can become that hopeful door through which we enter to gather more of God's promises. And when we do, God will be with us. He will protect and guide us and fight our battles. No other course is reasonable.

The Valley Between Bethel and Ai

After Achan and his accursed spoils had been burned in the Valley of Achor, God encouraged Joshua to take Ai. He even gave Joshua a battle plan. A contingency of Israelite soldiers was to lay in ambush behind the city while another contingency entered the valley between Bethel and Ai. The strategy was to draw out the men of Ai, then run away like they had before, causing the men of Ai to chase them. Meanwhile, those Israelites lying in ambush would enter the city and destroyed it. This happened as planned. Ai was captured and the fleeing Israelite army turned around and killed the men of Ai. After that, they went to Ai and killed the remaining inhabitants and burned the city. And this time God allowed them to keep the spoils.

That word "Ai" means, "a ruin, an overturned heap." And that city was referred to as The Heap or The Ruin after Israel's victory.

On the other hand, "Bethel" means, "house of God." It, too, was a Canaanite city. The site of several streams made it ideal for habitation. It was also a place where the Canaanites worshiped El, a generic name for god, before Baal worship became so pervasive. Thus, the land was once called El. Scripture tells us that in addition to the men of Ai, Joshua also fought the men of Bethel, for they joined Ai in warring against Israel. Joshua 8:17, *"And there was not a man left in Ai or Beth-el, that went not out after Israel: and they left the city open, and pursued after Israel."* But in the end, the Israelites vanquished them all.

Having to fight Bethel must have been disappointing for the Israelites on some level. Years before Joshua showed up, Jacob, while fleeing from his brother, Esau, stopped in El overnight and had a dream of a ladder reaching heaven. Because this was where Jacob encountered God, he called the place Bethel, house of God, referring to the God of Abraham, Isaac, and Jacob (Genesis 28:1-22). It was also the place he revisited when returning home after living in Syria for twenty years.

The return journey began after God identified Himself as *"the **God** of **Beth-el**, where thou anointedst the pillar, and where thou vowedst a vow unto me: now arise get thee out from this land, and return unto the land of thy kindred,* (Genesis 11:13)." Then in Genesis 35:1, God gave Jacob additional instructions. *"And God said unto Jacob, Arise, go up to **Beth-el**, and dwell there: and make there an altar unto God, that appeared unto thee when though fleddest from the face of Esau, they brother."*

Laban, Jacob's father-in-law, and Laban's sons were pagans, and some of their idols had found their way into Jacob's caravan. So, before going to Bethel, Jacob purged his household and buried both his wives' earrings and their idols under an oak tree in Shechem. Like the enslaved Israelites who would come long after and leave Egypt tainted by Egyptian beliefs, so Jacob's wives left Padanaram tainted with some of Laban's beliefs, beliefs that made them wear idol-inspired earrings and made Rachel steal her father's household gods.

When Jacob reached Bethel, God appeared to him, changed his name from Jacob to Israel, and restated the promises He had made to Abraham and Isaac. To seal his covenant with God, Jacob erected a stone pillar and consecrated it with a drink offering and oil.

Though Bethel was a holy place, we see that even in Joshua's time, it was also a place of enemies and idol worshippers. And it continued to be so even in Israel's later history when King Jeroboam, the first to rule the Northern Kingdom (10 tribes of Israel), had two golden calves constructed, then installed one in Dan and the other in Bethel.

Referring to the calf in Bethel, God, through Hosea, chastised the Israelites for their idolatry and foretold of coming judgment. Hosea 10:5 says, *"The inhabitants of Samaria shall fear because of the calves* (golden calves) *of **Bethaven**: for the people thereof shall mourn over it, and the priests thereof that rejoiced on it, for the glory thereof, because it is departed from it."* Here, instead of calling the place where the golden calf was located — Bethel, the house of God — Hosea called it Bethaven, "the house of vanity or house of iniquity." Idol worship had made Bethel a house of sin and wickedness.

How does that apply to us?

First, we must ask, "Can a house of God also become a house of vanity or house of idolatry?" The answer is obviously "Yes," since we have seen how it was so in the past. But what about the present? To that, also, we must answer, "Yes." And there is ample proof for anyone who cares to look. I covered this in my book, *The Coming Deception*, but will include some of it now.

The American church is in trouble. Without a revival, it will become more and more irrelevant as the days grow darker. Many churches no longer preach the full gospel. Instead, it's a watered-down version designed to offend no one. The words "sin" and "hell" are avoided.

Other churches are doing "Clown Communions" in which the pastor and congregation dress up as clowns. Still others are giving communion to their congregant's pets! There is even a "porn movie church" which shows an "R" rated film entitled, "Missionary Positions," under the guise of helping those addicted to porn. And who could believe there would ever be a nude church, where no one, including the pastor, wears clothes?

All show how far the church has fallen. Like Bethaven, it has become polluted and vain, with pastors enriching themselves and enjoying the limelight while having no accountability. They are shepherds who look after their own interests rather than their flock's. But sadly, many sheep follow them.

2 Timothy 4:3-4 warned of this. *"For the time will come when they will not endure sound doctrine; but after their own lusts shall they heap to themselves teachers, having itching ears; And they shall turn away their ears from the truth, and shall be turned unto fables."*

But praise God, there is still a remnant, those who believe in the full gospel of Jesus Christ. Unfortunately, as the days become more evil, believers may increasingly encounter false doctrine in their church, or sermonettes on things like, "how to become a better you;" all fluff and saccharin designed to fill "itching ears."

Already some solid Bible-believing churches have begun applying the world's standards by calling "good evil and evil good." Openly gays and lesbians are being ordained. Cohabitation between men and women is winked at and no longer called "fornication". Pornography is rampant, even among pastors. And sexual abuse of children at the hands of priests or ministers is being covered up. No longer the House of God, these churches have become a House of vanity or iniquity, and true believers must flee them and find a church that preaches the pure gospel without compromise.

But that's not the end. Even the remnant can be caught in the valley between Bethel and Ai. Ai, The Ruin, can be likened to the world's evil systems that are an abomination to God and, in turn, ruin lives. And when the remnant enters the valley to do (spiritual) battle there may be those in Bethaven, those "religious" people who have compromised with the world, and "go along to get along," who come against them. And instead of having their backs, these religious people attack them.

These days it would be well to be reminded of what happened to the church in Hitler's Germany. Instead of standing against tyranny and lies, little by little it caved to the corrupt Nazi system and even ended up supporting it. From Bethel it became Bethaven.

It's the church of Laodicea, the church that Jesus will spew out of His mouth. And many are in that valley, standing between them and Ai, heartbroken and disappointed that they must battle them both.

It is, indeed, a sad valley to be in. But may the remnant rise up and be encouraged in the Lord. And if they follow God's battle plan, they, like Joshua, will prevail.

Valley of Ajalon

Ajalon lies between Jericho and the Mediterranean Sea. And in this valley of plentiful pastureland, something incredible happened. After hearing how the Israelites had vanquished Jericho and Ai, the Gibeonites, fearing they would be next, tricked Joshua into making a peace treaty with them. Though they were local, they claimed to be from a faraway land. Deceived, and without consulting God, Joshua and Israel's leaders swore an oath to the Gibeonites that they would not make war with them. This was a direct violation of God's instructions, for He had ordered Joshua to destroy all the inhabitants in the Promised Land.

Now, bound to their oath, the Israelites could do nothing but abide by it. So, when the local Amorite kings became fearful of what Gibeon's alliance to Israel would mean to their own safety, they attacked Gibeon. Immediately, Gibeon sent word to Joshua requesting help. And Joshua and his army did, indeed, come to the rescue. (Joshua 10:1-14)

Even though Joshua had violated God's command, God was merciful and the slaughter of the Amorites, at the hands of Joshua's men, was great. But God didn't stop there. He sent hailstones. Joshua 10:11 says, *"they were more which died with hailstones than they whom the children of Israel slew with the sword."* Interestingly, even now, small stones, foreign to this valley, can still be found there. Local geologists assert they are little meteorites.

And there's more. In order to have enough daylight to thoroughly defeat the Amorites, Joshua, with incredible faith, ordered the sun and moon to stand still. And God backed him up! *"And the sun stood still, and the moon stayed, until the people* (Israel) *had avenged themselves upon their enemies* (the Amorites) . . . *So the sun stood still in the midst of heaven, and hasted not to go down about a whole day,"* Joshua 10:13.

This is a valley of miracles, for only the hand of God could do such a thing. And it's a valley that someday we may find ourselves in because God is still a God of miracles. There may be times, in the midst of our battles, when God will do something supernatural. That cancer disappears without treatment; that blind eye can see; money, from an unknown source, suddenly appears in our checking account or mailbox; a person who has been dead and lying in a casket for hours, suddenly awakens. I have heard actual testimonies of all these things. And God is no respecter of persons. What He can do for one He can do for all.

But notice that great faith was in operation. Joshua, in Joshua 10:12, said the following **before** the miracle. *"Then spake Joshua to the LORD in the day when the LORD delivered up the Amorites before the children of Israel, and he* (Joshua) *said in the sight of Israel, Sun, stand thou still upon Gibeon; and thou, Moon, in the valley of Ajalon."* Prior to it even happening, Joshua declared it. Had God instructed him to do this? Scripture doesn't say. But Joshua made the proclamation public, in front of his men. And that took incredible faith. Having the sun and moon stand still was a tall order, something only God could do, yet Joshua confidently declared it.

Sometimes, this kind of extraordinary faith is necessary before we see such a great miracle. But sometimes it's not. Sometimes it just happens when we are simply trusting God to move in our lives and are patiently waiting for Him to act. I've heard of it happening both ways. And though faith is involved in each, it doesn't necessarily mean we have to be "super heroes of faith" before we get our miracle because Jesus said in Matthew 17:20, *"If ye have faith as a grain of mustard seed ye shall say unto this mountain, Remove hence to yonder place: and it shall remove; and nothing shall be impossible unto you."* Mustard seeds are small, so yes, even our little faith can get God's attention. What's more, God is merciful and gracious and always exceeds our expectations.

When we need it the most, may we all experience the Valley of Ajalon in our lives!

Valley of Hinnom

Historians disagree on its exact location, but all acknowledge it was a valley right outside Jerusalem. Also called the Valley of the son of Hinnom and The Valley, it was terrifying and shameful, for it was the site of child sacrifices, the place where parents sometimes took their first-born infants and sacrificed them to Molech or Baal.

Though difficult to imagine such cruelty or barbarity, and as horrible as it sounds, the babies were placed into the burning belly of Molech and made to *"pass through the fire."* Even Israel's kings Ahaz (2 Chronicles 28:3) and Manasseh (2 Chronicles 33:6) offered their children. It took King Josiah to put an end to it (2 Kings 23:10). *"And he* (Josiah) *defiled Topheth* (which means oven, the burning place, abomination) *which is in the **valley of the children of Hinnom**, that no man might make his* *son or his daughter to pass through the fire to Molech."* What Josiah did was desecrate the area so that no one would go there to sacrifice their children anymore. How he did it, the Bible doesn't say. Perhaps he scattered bones of the dead over the ground. But whatever it was, it put a stop to it.

God, in Jeremiah 2:23, tells Israel they are polluted for this great sin. *"How canst thou say, I* (Israel) *am not **polluted**, I have not gone after Baalim* (Baal)*? see thy way in the valley* (of Hinnom) *know what thou hast done* (offered their children to idols)*."* Despite their protests and claims of fidelity, God knew what they were doing, and He wasn't about to let them off the hook.

It's important to understand how serious the shedding of innocent blood is to God and how it pollutes the land. To do so, we must digress. This fundamental truth was asserted by God early on in Israel's history. Let's look at it.

After Cain killed his brother, Abel, God, in Genesis 4:10, asked Cain, *"What hast thou done? **the voice of thy brother's blood crieth unto me from the ground.**"* That word "voice" in Hebrew means, "call aloud, a voice, a sound." Here, blood is equated with life, having its own voice and speaking a sound or language that God can hear as it cries out for justice. That's why, in Genesis 9:5-6, God commanded that if a man or beast took the life of a man, the blood of that man or beast would be required. And He stated His reason. *"Whoso sheddeth man's blood, by man shall his blood be shed: for in the image of God made he man."* Only blood was payment for blood because man was made in God's image. This command is repeated throughout the Old Testament.

Numbers 35:30-33 gives additional insight. *"Whoso killeth any person, the murderer shall be put to death by the mouth of witnesses: but one witness shall not testify against any person to cause him to die* (Here the criteria was set up that it must take at least two witnesses to convict a murderer) *Moreover ye shall take no satisfaction* (ransom) *for the life of a murderer, which is guilty of death; but he shall surely be put to death. And you shall accept no satisfaction* (ransom) *for him that is fled to the city of his refuge, that he should come again to dwell in the land, until the death of the* (high) *priest. So ye shall not **pollute** the land wherein ye are: for blood it **defileth** the land: and **the land cannot be cleansed of the blood that is shed therein, but by the blood of him that shed it.** Defile not therefore* *the land which ye shall inhabit, wherein among the children of Israel."* This clearly spells out what happens when murderers are not put to death. *We pollute and defile our land.*

Regarding witnesses, Deuteronomy 19:18-21 adds this: *"And the judges shalt make diligent inquisition: and, behold, if the **witness** be a false witness, and hath testified falsely against his brother; Then shall ye do unto him, as he had thought to have done unto his brother: so shalt thou put the evil away from among you. And those which remain shall hear, and fear, and shall henceforth commit no more any such evil among you. **And thine eye shall not pity**; but life shall go for life, eye for eye, tooth for tooth, hand for hand, foot for foot* (the punishment must fit the crime)."

Further instruction is given in Deuteronomy 19:11-13. *"But if any man hate his neighbour, and lie in wait for him, and rise up against him, and smite him mortally that he die, and fleeth into one of these cities* (cities of refuge—which was only for accidental killings) *Then the elders of his city shall send and fetch him thence, and deliver him into the hand of the avenger of blood, that he may die. **Thine eye shall not pity him**,* (God calls us to walk, not in sentimentality, but in His ways, His laws) *but* *thou shalt put away the guilt of innocent blood from Israel,* **that it may go well with thee.** "

So, if the guilt of innocent blood is not put away, meaning the murderer is not put to death, it not only pollutes the land, but it will not go well with that nation.

From these few Scriptures we know that 1) God Himself instituted the death penalty. 2) That only blood can pay for the shedding of innocent blood. 3) A murderer must be convicted by at least two witnesses. 4) If a witness falsely testifies against someone on charges of murder, then that witness must forfeit his life. 5) If a murderer does not pay with his blood that land becomes defiled/polluted and it will not go well for that nation. 6) We are not to pity the murderer. 7) The execution of a murderer will serve as a deterrent against further evil.

Obviously, our justice system doesn't follow all these ordinances of God. And that begs this question. What will happen to a people and land that is polluted by the shedding of innocent blood?

Both words—pollute and defileth—in Numbers 35:30-33 are the same word in Hebrew, *chaneph,* and means, "to soil in a moral sense, to greatly profane." I don't think it's difficult to see how morally soiled we are as a nation. And a morally soiled nation will not prosper.

God, in Leviticus 18:25, warns what will happen to a nation that has defiled its land. *"And the land is defiled: therefore **I do visit the iniquity thereof upon it, and the land itself vomiteth out her inhabitants.**"*

When murder (the shedding of innocent blood either by a man/woman killing another in cold blood or by the act of abortion) is not covered by blood then God is bound by His word to act as the blood avenger Himself and rectify it.

As previously mentioned, blood has a voice and innocent blood will cry out for God's justice. When it does, God will act. First, by visiting *"the iniquity thereof upon it."* In other words, He will lift His hand of protection and blessing from that nation and that nation will literally reap what it has sown.

And this judgment could come in the same way it did when Babylon "slaughtered" Israel in the Valley of Hinnom, the very place the Israelites slaughtered their own children. So, we see that judgment could come through wars. But it could also come through civil unrest and government corruption.

Then next, He will allow the land itself to vomit out its inhabitants through natural disasters. I don't believe it's any accident that our nation has had so many natural disasters in the past several years. Statistics reveal natural disasters are on the increase. Our land is vomiting us out. Expect more of this in the future.

The world has innocent blood on its hands. Like those Israelites who sacrificed their babies in the Valley of Hinnom, so we have, in our day slaughtered our babies through abortion. And the abortion situation alone is enough to allow God to destroy us utterly. I believe it's only due to His incredible mercy that we have not suffered more.

But that was Old Testament. Right? Certainly, Jesus changed everything. Yes, grace changed everything, but Jesus did NOT do away with capital punishment. It still stands as part of His law. Murder is still forbidden in the New Testament (Matthew 19:18, Romans 13:9, 1Peter 4:15, 1 John 3:15).

Next, according to Malachi 3:6, God changes not. And Hebrews 13:8 says that Jesus is the same yesterday, today and forever. Considering the above, we see that God had not changed His mind. The same blood criteria applies to murder in the New Testament.

Jesus did not come to destroy the law but to fulfill it. In Matthew 5:17-18, He said, *"Think not that I am come to destroy the law, or the prophets: I am not come to destroy, but to fulfil. For verily I say unto you, Till heaven and earth pass, **one jot or one tittle shall in no wise pass from the law, till all be fulfilled.**"*

But certainly a "new" dispensation has come with the "new" covenant? Yes, as previously mentioned, it is grace. Having said that, is there no way out in the New Testament for murderers other than the death penalty? Let's take a look.

First, it's important to remember that the Old Testament Scriptures we looked at regarding murder were Scriptures in which God was speaking to Moses, who represented the law or authority or the government, and as such He was laying down the pattern to be followed by a nation. In other words, God was establishing national law (for Israel and all future Godly nations).

But when Jesus spoke to individuals, a different standard was applied. Throughout Matthew chapter 5, during the sermon on the mount, Jesus talked to the multitudes. Matthew 5:1-2 says, *"And seeing the **multitudes**, he went up into a mountain: and when he was set, his disciples came unto him: And he opened his mouth and taught them, saying..."* Jesus wasn't speaking to the lawmakers/authority/government. Rather, He was speaking to the masses, the common man. The substance of what He said also makes it clear that He was addressing two distinct groups of people: 1) the law breaker or criminal and 2) the victim of crime.

Let's first look at what He said to the "criminals," those breakers of God's laws. Matthew 5:21-24, *"Ye have heard that **it was said by them of old time**, Thou shalt not kill; and whosoever shall kill shall be in danger of the judgment: But I say unto you, That **whosoever is angry with his brother without a cause** shall be in danger of the judgment: and whosoever shall say to his brother, Raca, shall be in danger of the council; but whosoever shall say, Thou fool, shall be in danger of hell fire."*

Jesus began by reminding them of the law during Old Testament times. The law said, Thou shalt not kill. However, under the "new" Testament, Jesus is coming down even harder. He said if you're angry with your brother for no reason, or if you speak evil of him, you're in danger of judgment. Jesus raised the standard. He didn't lower it. He was saying that hatred and slander are akin to murder.

Then look what He said about adultery: Matthew 5:27-28 *"Ye have heard that **it was said by them of old time**, Thou shalt not commit adultery: But I say unto you, That whosoever looketh on a woman to lust after her hath committed adultery with her already in his heart."*

Again, Jesus mentioned "old time" referring to the Old Testament days when the admonition was not to commit adultery. But now, under the "new" order of things, just looking at someone with lust constituted adultery. Again, Jesus was raising the bar. He was telling criminals, those breakers of God's law, that the standards are even higher than they had previously thought!

Now, let's look at the second group Jesus addressed—the victims of crime. Jesus said in Matthew 5:38-41, *"Ye have heard that it hath been said, An eye for an eye, and a tooth for a tooth: But I say unto you, That ye resist not evil: but whosoever shall smite thee on thy right cheek, turn to him the other also. And if any man will sue thee at the law, and take away thy coat, let him have thy cloke also. And whosoever shall compel thee to go a mile, go with him twain."*

This Scripture is used by many to justify the abolition of the death penalty. Because of Jesus' seemingly lenient attitude toward evildoers, they believe He abolished that penalty. Nothing could be further from the truth. In Matthew 5:38-41, Jesus was not speaking to criminals but to their victims.

He told them that previously the standard was an eye for an eye (a just punishment to fit the crime). But now, don't look for revenge or retaliation, but forgive, forgive, forgive! If someone steals your shirt, give him your coat, too (forgive, forgive, forgive). And if someone forces you to go a mile with him, don't just stop there, go two. Jesus was saying that the victim's attitude (NOT the state's attitude or the law's attitude or the government's attitude) toward the criminal must now be one of forgiveness, meekness, and forbearance.

Finally, we come to grace. We know sinners are saved by grace and that the blood of Jesus covers their sins. So, if someone murders (sheds innocent blood) and comes into the saving knowledge of Jesus and repents and puts that sin under the blood, then the blood requirement of the blood avenger is fulfilled. Jesus' blood, in that instance, is the perfect fulfilling of the law. Jesus' blood becomes the substitute for the blood of the actual murderer. His blood appeases the outcry of the innocent blood that was shed. And His blood appeases God the Father's sense of justice.

However, when a murderer has NOT come to the Lord, has not put his murder under the blood of Jesus, then the blood requirement still stands. That person is, in effect, under the law — the Old Testament law—and his blood is required. If that blood requirement is not met, then it contributes to the defilement of the land.

Now, returning to the Valley of Hinnom: God instructed Jeremiah to call Israel to repentance and He recited a litany of their offences. Included in them were child sacrifices to Molech and God's decree of coming judgment. Jeremiah 7:31-33, "*And they* (Israel) *have built the high places of Tophet, which is in the **valley of the***

son of Hinnom, to burn their sons and their daughters in the fire; which I commanded them not, neither came it into my heart. Therefore, behold, the days come, saith the LORD, that it shall no more be called Tophet, nor the valley of the son of Hinnom, but the valley of slaughter: for they shall bury in Tophet, till there be no place. And the carcases of this people shall be meat for the fowls of the heaven, and for the beasts of the earth; and none shall fray them away." God, again, repeated this promised judgment for their sins at Hinnom in Jeremiah 19:2-15.

Judgment, indeed, was coming. The Israelites had shed innocent blood, now their blood would be shed. As mentioned, this happened during the Babylonian conquest when many Israelites were "slaughtered" in the Hinnom valley.

But oh, how merciful God is! Though judgment was coming, He promised to restore Israel in Jeremiah 31:40. *"And the whole valley of the dead bodies, and of the ashes* (the valley of Hinnom) *and all the fields unto the brook of Kidron, unto the corner of the horse gate toward the east, shall be holy unto the LORD; it shall not be plucked up, nor thrown down any more for ever."* At a future time, God would forgive and restore not only the people but the land. And they would be His forever. And that will occur after the seven-year Tribulation when God makes Israel the head of nations.

The Hinnom valley became symbolic for sin and the corrupt world system, as well as a place of misery and eternal punishment. After it was desecrated by King Josiah, it became a place where dead animals and criminals were burned in a fire that never went out. It's a picture of hell and the future judgment that awaits unrepented sinners who refuse to accept Jesus as their Savior.

Indeed, that word "Gehenna," a corruption of the word "Hinnom," became one of the words for hell in Greek. The Greek translation is actually *"geenna,"* and literally means, "valley of the son of Hinnom" illustrating that even in the New Testament, Hinnom was still symbolic of hell and destruction.

Below are some verses where *geenna* is used in the New Testament.

In Matthew 5:22, Jesus said, *"But I say to you, That whosoever is angry with his brother without a cause shall be in danger of the judgment: and whosoever shall say to his brother, Raca, shall be in danger of the council: but whosoever shall say, Thou fool, shall be in danger of* **hell** (*geenna*/Gehenna) *fire."*

Then Jesus said in Matthew 5:29, *"And if thy right eye offend thee, pluck it out, and cast it from thee: for it is profitable for thee that one of thy members should perish, and not that thy whole body should be cast in* **hell** (*geenna*/Gehenna)." This is repeated in Matthew 18:9.

Again, Jesus is speaking in Matthew 10:28. *"And fear not them which kill the body, but are not able to kill the soul: but rather fear him* (God) *which is able to destroy both soul and body in* **hell** (*geenna*, Gehenna)." Jesus repeats this in Luke 12:5.

Jesus said, *"Woe unto you, scribes and Pharisees, hypocrites! for ye compass sea and land to make one proselyte, and when he is made, ye make him twofold more the child of* **hell** (*geenna*/Gehenna) *than yourselves,"* (Matthew 23:15).

A few verses later, Jesus tells these scribes and Pharisees, *"Ye serpents, ye generation of vipers, how can ye escape the damnation of* **hell** (geenna, Gehenna)?" (Matthew 23:33)

103

In Mark 9:43-48, Jesus said, *"And if thy hand offend thee, cut it off: it is better for thee to enter into life maimed, than having two hands to go into **hell** (geenna/Gehenna), into the fire that never shall be quenched. Where their worm dieth not, and the fire is not quenched, And if thy foot offend thee, cut it off: it is better for thee to enter halt into life, than having two feet to be cast into hell (geenna/Gehenna) into the fire that never shall be quenched. Where their worm dieth not, and the fire is not quenched. And if thine eye offend thee, pluck it out: it is better for thee to enter into the kingdom of God with one eye, than having two eyes to be cast into **hell** (geenna,* Gehenna) *fire: Where their worm dieth not, and the fire is not quenched."*

Those who don't believe in hell need to understand that Jesus spent more time talking about it than anyone else. Note, it is Jesus Himself Who is describing hell in these Scriptures. Why? Because He doesn't want anyone to go there. It's a terrible place. And like the valley of Hinnom outside Jerusalem's gates, which burned constantly and was made foul by dead bodies, so, the fires of hell will never go out and it, too, is filled with the spiritually dead.

Because Jesus paid for our sins, this is a valley no one should ever enter. But sadly, those who reject the salvation that only comes through Jesus will enter it. It will be their abode for all eternity.

But is there anything that would necessitate believers going there? After all, the blood of Jesus covers all our sins so we don't have to pay for them ourselves. True. But there possibly is one thing that can take a believer to this valley. I have covered it in my book, *12 Questions New Christians Frequently Ask*, but will repeat it here in its entirety because of its importance. It's referring to a Christian being blotted out of the Lamb's Book of Life, the book that contains the name of every believer allowed to enter the kingdom of heaven.

How can a genuine Christian be blotted out? (pages 159-163)

I want to tread carefully here. God's grace is an incredibly wonderful thing. His blood pays for all our sins: past, present, and future. And there is no sin too great God can't or won't forgive if we confess it and repent. But I fear that the current teaching of "hyper grace" can lead believers astray. Grace does not give us license to live anyway we want. God is holy and we, too, are called to live holy lives, submitted and obedient to Him.

Galatians 6:7 says, *"Be not deceived; God is not mocked: for whatsoever a man soweth, that shall he also reap."* There is no fooling God. Our fruits will always give us away.

But can a genuine Christian, one who isn't perfect but who loves God and tries to live a holy life, go to hell? I believe the one thing that can derail a genuine Christian is unforgiveness and perhaps even keep him from heaven. Why? Because Jesus Himself said, *"For **if ye forgive** men their trespasses, your heavenly Father will also forgive you; But **if ye forgive not** men their trespasses, neither will your Father forgive your trespasses,"* Matthew 6:14-15.

The whole reason we, as born-again believers, have assurance of heaven is that we are forgiven, and our sins are covered by the blood of Jesus. But here, Jesus is saying that our sins are **NOT** forgiven if we don't forgive others.

Again, in Matthew 18:23-35 Jesus talks about a king who began tallying the accounts of his servants. One servant owed him a great deal of money, yet the king forgave him his debt. But this same servant, who was owed a small sum by a fellow servant, refused to forgive that servant. Jesus then, in verse 34, tells how the king reacted. *"And his lord was wroth, and delivered him* (the servant who had owed him a lot of money) *to the tormentors, till he should pay all that was due unto him."*

In Mark 11:25-26, Jesus said, *"And when ye stand praying, **forgive**, if ye have ought against any: that your Father also which is in heaven may **forgive** you your trespasses. But if ye do not **forgive**, neither will your Father which is in heaven **forgive** your trespasses."* If our sins are not forgiven by God then we are considered sinners, and no sinner will enter the kingdom of heaven!

Jesus continued this theme in Luke 6:37. *"Judge not, and ye shall not be judged: condemn not, and ye shall not be condemned: **forgive**, and ye shall be forgiven."*

When Jesus taught His disciples the Lord's prayer, He said in Luke 11:4, *"And **forgive us** our sins; **for we also forgive every one** that is indebted to us."* Again, God's forgiving us is tied into us forgiving others. No forgiveness for others, then no forgiveness for us.

Revelation 3:5 is sobering. In it, Jesus said, *"He that overcometh, the same shall be clothed in white raiment; and I will not **blot out** his name out of the book of life."* Here, Jesus indicates it's possible to be blotted out of the book of life. And what then? *"Whosoever was not found written in the book of life was cast into the lake of fire."* Let that not happen to us because of unforgiveness!

We have no right to keep grudges or maintain a heart of unforgiveness. Jesus is like that king in Matthew 18 who has forgiven us much (a large sum). Therefore, how can we not forgive others their small sum? It's up to God to settle the accounts. Romans 12:19b says, *"Vengeance is mine; I Will repay, saith the Lord."* So, let's leave it to Him.

While I was struggling with this issue, I happened to see a Christian program where an African pastor was relaying an amazing story, a story which was documented and certified by his community.

He had had an argument with his wife and had been rejecting her apologies, refusing to forgive her as well as punishing her with the silent treatment for nearly a week. At the end of it, he had a terrible car accident resulting in a death experience and found himself in hell.

He described the horror of it and how he cried out to God that this had to be a mistake. He was a pastor and a true lover of God. An angel appeared to him and told him if God were to leave him in this state of death, hell would be his eternal home. Because he refused to forgive his wife, God could not forgive him. The pastor immediately repented and found himself on a slab in the morgue.

We are not required or expected to accept every Christian's supernatural experience as fact, so believe or not as you will. But it does give food for thought as well as give the above Scriptures a startling and horrifying sense of realism.

As Christians, we are called to repentance and to forgive those who offend us, and doing so will help keep us out of the Valley of Hinnom.

Valley of the Giants

The Promised Land was full of giants. But long before Joshua and his army came to claim their inheritance, these giants were attempting to thwart God's plan. This has been covered extensively in my book entitled, *The Coming Deception*, and is too long to repeat here. But for the sake of clarity, I will mention a few points.

First, we know from Genesis 3:15 that the Seed, Jesus, would crush Satan's head through His death on the cross, thereby redeeming mankind. But it also talks about another seed, Satan's. In both cases "seed" is the same word *zera* and refers to a physical seed. Here, God predicted Satan would also have a physical seed. His seed would become part of a diabolical scheme to corrupt the seed of woman and prevent the Deliverer from coming to crush him.

We see his plan unfold in Genesis 6:1-4. *"And it came to pass, when men began to multiply on the face of the earth, and daughters were born unto them, That the sons of God saw the daughters of men that they were fair; and they took them wives of all which they chose . . . There were giants in the earth in those days; and also after that, when the sons of God came in unto the daughters of men, and they bare children to them, the same became mighty men which were of old, men of renown."*

So, fallen angels physically took women as wives and had children, creating what the Bible calls, the Nephilim. In addition to cohabitating with women, *Jasher* (an ancient text that was quoted by Joshua and Samuel in the Old Testament) also claimed these angels comingled the seed of different animals, creating hybrids and corrupting the earth. But it doesn't end there. Many clues suggest that angels also comingled their seed with animals to create chimeras. Cave drawings and petroglyphs of chimeras can be seen in nearly every ancient culture around the world, including America.

The result of all this was chaos and the acceleration of evil. To preserve the Messianic blood line, God had to wipe out all corrupt human flesh by sending a flood. At the same time, He wiped out all the animals the Nephilim had polluted through crossbreeding. God would start over through Noah, his offspring, and the animals Noah took with him on the ark.

Genesis 6:9 tells us that, *"Noah was a just man and perfect in his generations, and Noah walked with God."* It's interesting to note that word "perfect" in Hebrew is *tamiym* and means, "without blemish, complete, full, whole, undefiled, upright, healthy, **soundness of flesh**." Though Noah was just and upright in the eyes of God, *tamiym* denotes physical, not spiritual, purity. It indicated his flesh was sound. He was 100% human. His DNA had not been corrupted.

The ancient Israelites understood this and knew Genesis 6:1-4 meant fallen angels and that their offspring were the giants. And this was believed up to and including Jesus' day as well as during the early years of the church.

Additionally, Flavius Josephus wrote about this unholy cohabitation between angels and women in his *Jewish Antiquities*, claiming that the giants' offspring were the Titans and Olympians in Greek mythology. Enoch also wrote of them in his *Book of Enoch* and *Book of the Giants*. And many early church fathers wrote about giants as well, including Clement of Rome (Pope from 88 A.D. to 99 A.D.); Tertullian (early Christian theologian, around 200 A.D.); Justin Martyr (100A.D. – 165A.D., Christian teacher); Irenaeus (125-202 A.D., Greek cleric who combated heresy); Lactantius (250 A.D. – 325 A.D.; early Christian author); and Ambrose (339 A.D. – 397 A.D., Archbishop of Milan in 4th Century).

Giants are even mentioned in some of the Apocrypha, such as the *Book of Wisdom, Baruch,* and *Maccabees.*

Notice, Genesis 6:4 tells us that this incursion happened twice, indicating it occurred before the flood as well as after. How this second infiltration occurred is too lengthy to go into. But because these giants were hybrids, neither fully angelic nor fully human, they were an abomination to God. And when Israel entered the Promised Land, God ordered them to utterly destroy these unholy offspring. It's interesting to note that even today, many in the Illuminati claim to be descendants of the Nephilim.

The Valley of the Giants is mentioned in Joshua 15:8, 18:16; 2 Samuel 5:18, 22; 2 Samuel 23:13; 1

Chronicles 11:15, 14:19,13; and Isaiah 17:5. It was often the site of conflict.

The giants, those encountered by the Israelites, were called by many names, including Rephaim, Zamzummim, Emim, and Anakim. But what were they like? Genesis 6:1-4 gives us insight into their progenitors, the Nephilim. In these verses they are called, "giants, mighty men, and men of renown." Breaking it down gives further clues of their nature and character. That word "giants" means, "the **fallen ones, bully or tyrant.**" "Mighty" means, "powerful, warrior, tyrant and **to rise oneself up in arrogance and stand in God's face.**" And "men" in "men of renown" means, "frail, feeble, sick, desperately wicked, mortal." While "renown" means, "to mark or brand."

Putting it together we get a picture of what these angelic offspring were like: They were the fallen ones. They were powerful. They acted as bullies and tyrants. They were arrogant and defied God. But now mortal, they were feeble and frail in contrast to their former state. And it suggests that they were marked or branded by God.

According to Scripture, the giants Joshua encountered had similar traits. They were huge, strong, tyrants, bullies and many were cannibals, a fact that modern archeology has confirmed in such places as Chaco Canyon, New Mexico. Numbers 13:32 also hints at this. *"The land, through which we* (the Israelite spies) *have gone to search it, is a land that **eateth up the inhabitants** thereof."* These giants also had unique physical characteristics such as double rows of teeth, six fingers on each hand and six toes on each foot.

They were a formidable enemy, but God gave the Israelites the victory. One example is Hebron, a giant stronghold that was completely vanquished. Here's what Josephus said about that massacre: *"When they* (the Israelites) *had taken it* (Hebron), *they slew all the inhabitants. There were till then left the race of giants, who had bodies so large and countenances to entirely different from other men, that they were amazing to the sight and terrible to the hearing. The bones of these men are still shown to this very day, unlike any credible relations of other men."*

Over and over again, God gave His people victory despite great odds. Even years later, we see God give David, a young shepherd boy with a sling shot and pebble, victory over the giant, Goliath. It shows how little we bring to the fight and how much God brings.

Anyone who thinks that after coming to the Lord they will never face another problem is sadly mistaken. Like the Israelites who entered the Promised Land only to encounter giants, so we, too, will, sooner or later, find ourselves in the Valley of Giants.

Yes, we have overcome that one giant of our past that stood barring the entrance to the Promised Land. But who would have thought we would face more giants once we got there? They seem to be everywhere. Though they will be different for everyone, they are the giants that try to keep us from our inheritance; that try to keep us from God's promises. Hardship, sickness, relationship problems, battle fatigue, disappointment with God, death of a loved one, financial issues, loss of a job, the list is endless, but all conspire to keep us from the full life Jesus promised when He said He had come that we may have life and *"have it more abundantly,"* John 10:10. The Amplified says it this way: *"I came that they may have and enjoy life, and have it in abundance to the full, till it overflows."*

117

Satan placed giants in the Promised Land to thwart God's pledge to Israel regarding His promise that they would become a great nation and have their own land. In the same way, Satan places giants in our land to thwart the promises God has made us. In the face of every giant, we must stay the course and fight the good fight of faith. But it's not always easy.

I must confess I have whined to God, asking Him where was this "abundant, overflowing life"? Those were the times when my giants seemed too strong to conquer; when they seemed they were getting the upper hand. Those were the times when I became "weary of well doing;" when the end goal seemed out of reach. But God . . . . Oh, how wonderful He is! Like the cavalry, He is never late and so able to rescue, refresh, restore, and push us over the finish line.

I love the movie *Facing the Giants* because it's a great metaphor for living life in Christ. It's the story about a mediocre high school football team that, through hard work, sacrifice and a new mind set where they decided to honor God rather than themselves, made it all the way to the state finals and there had to face the team that had held the championship title for years.

This champion team was larger, stronger, and more skilled yet the smaller team prevailed.

In the same way, our giants may be larger, stronger, and more powerful than we are, but with God nothing is impossible. If only we believed that and lived that, we would always be victorious in the Valley of the Giants. May it be so!

Valley of Jezreel

I call this the Valley of the Unexpected. It was here that Israel won a great victory in a most unusual way. Here's the story.

Because of Israel's many sins, God judged them by allowing the Midianites to oppress them for seven years (Judges 6:1). Life was difficult. The Midianites stole their crops and possessions. Poverty was widespread. Remember, seven in the Bible is the number of perfection or completion. So, at the end of seven years Israel's judgment was complete, and God sent an angel to Gideon instructing him to deliver his people.

Gideon was a timid man, an unlikely hero, just the type God loves to use. After much hesitation, Gideon obeyed and assembled an army of 32,000, then encamped in the valley of Harod. Imagine his surprise when God told him in Judges 7:2, *"The people that are with thee are too many for me* (God) *to give the Midianites into their hands, lest Israel vaunt themselves against me, saying Mine own hand hath saved me."* God then ordered Gideon to weed them out by telling those who were afraid, to return home. That created an exodus of 22,000, leaving only 10,000.

God still wasn't satisfied and said in Judges 7:4 (Amplified), *"The men are still too many; bring them down to the water, and I will test them for you there. And he of whom I say to you, This man shall go with you, shall go with you; and he of whom I say to you, This man shall not go with you, shall not go."*

At this point was Gideon getting nervous or wondering what in the world God was doing? The Bible doesn't say. It just says he obeyed and took his remaining troops to a stream, and per God's instructions, told them to drink. Those who dipped their hands in the water then lapped the water from their hands like a dog where the ones God chose. The rest were also sent home. Now only 300 remained.

I think I'd be shaking in my sandals by now because the Midianites and their allies had arrived and were camped in the valley of Jezreel. And according to Judges 7:12, their force was intimidating. *"And the Midianites and the Amalekites and all the children of the east lay along in the valley* (of Jezreel) *like **grasshoppers** for multitude; and their camels were without number, as the sand by the sea side for multitude."* When grasshoppers (locusts) descend upon an area, they cover the land like a blanket. Their numbers are too great to count. So is the sand on a beach. Here, Judges 7:12 is painting a bleak picture of overwhelming odds.

Still, Gideon stayed the course, even when God instructed him and his army to carry trumpets, pitchers, and torches rather than weapons.

Could things get any worse? Yes, because then God told Gideon to have his meager army ring the camp of the enemy at night. Again, Gideon obeyed and, per God's orders, did the following according to Judges 7:16-18, *"he divided the three hundred men into three companies, and he put a trumpet in every man's hand, with empty pitchers, and lamps within the pitchers. And he said unto them, Look on me, and do likewise: and, behold, when I come to the outside of the camp, it shall be that, as I do, so shall ye do. When I blow with a trumpet, I and all that are with me, then blow ye the trumpets also on every side of all the camp, and say, The sword of the LORD, and of Gideon."*

Verse 20 goes on to say, *"And the three companies blew the trumpets, and brake the pitchers, and held the lamps* (they were lit) *in their left hands, and the trumpets in their right hands to blow withal: and they cried, The sword of the LORD, and of Gideon."*

Notice, that because their hands were full, it was impossible for the Israelites to defend themselves. I think supernatural faith and courage were in operation here, enabling this small band to not only face such a superior force, but to do it, unarmed.

What happened next? The trumpets and burning torches caused such confusion in the enemy's camp that they began killing each other and ultimately fled. Then Gideon gathered additional forces and pursued the Midianites and their allies to achieve a great victory.

What does that say to us? Yes, God is great. He can do anything. And yes, nothing is impossible for Him. And yes, faith and obedience are critical for victory. But it also says that when we are in the midst of strife or contention, for that is what the word "Midian" means, expect the unexpected from God. He may not act or come through in the way we think or imagine. We can't put Him in a box. We must allow Him to have His way and not shrink back or give up just because it's not how we would do it or how we imagined God should do it. His remedy may be something unthinkable or incredible. And like Gideon, we need to accept this, and allow Him to be God.

Isaiah 55:8-9 tells us that God's ways aren't our ways. *"For my* (God's) *thoughts are not your thoughts, neither are your ways my ways, saith the LORD, For as the heavens are higher than the earth, so are my ways higher than your ways, and my thoughts than your thoughts."*

God knows just what to do in every situation and what the perfect solution or remedy would be. He is an exciting God. Like Gideon, we need to let God have His way in our lives, then expect the unexpected as He creatively handles things.

To God be the glory! He truly is amazing!

Valley of Sorek

This valley is a cautionary tale. It involves the downfall of Samson, a hero and judge of Israel.

Once again, Israel's many sins caused God to give them into the hands of their enemies. This time it was the Philistines, and it was for forty years. But, as usual, God's mercy finally prevailed over judgment. At the end of forty years, an angel of the Lord appeared to Manoah's baren wife. They were from the tribe of Dan and lived along the border between the Danites and Philistines.

The angel came with wonderful news. She would have a son, and he would be special. As a Nazarite, dedicated to God, he would deliver Israel from the Philistines. But there was a catch. In Judges 13:5, the angel told her, *"For, lo, thou shalt conceive, and bear a son; and no razor shall come on his head: for the child shall be a Nazarite unto God from the womb: and he shall begin to deliver Israel out of the hand of the Philistines."*

According to Numbers 6:1-8, being a Nazarite came with three prohibitions. Not only could her son never cut his hair, he could not eat grapes or drink wine or alcohol, or contaminate himself by touching a dead body or any unclean thing. *"And the LORD spake unto Moses, saying, Speak unto the children of Israel, and say unto them, When either man or woman shall separate themselves to vow a vow of a Nazarite, to separate themselves unto the LORD: He shall separate himself from wine and strong drink, and shall drink no vinegar of wine, or vinegar of strong drink, neither shall he drink any liquor of grapes, nor eat moist grapes, or dried. All the days of his separation shall he eat nothing that is made of the vine tree, from the kernels even to the husk. All the days of the vow of his separation there shall no razor come upon his head: until the days be fulfilled, in the which he separateth himself unto the LORD, he shall be holy, and shall let the locks of the hair of his head grow. All the days that he separateth himself unto the LORD he shall come at no dead body. He shall not make himself unclean for his father, or for his mother, for his brother, or for his sister, when they die: because the consecration of his God is upon his head. All the days of his separation he is holy unto the LORD."*

So, Samson, the Nazarite, was born. His name means, "sun, sunlight, sun rising, be brilliant and a notched battlement." Some historians believe that because Samson's name was derived from the word *"shemesh"* and he was born only a few miles from Beth-Shemesh, meaning, "house of the sun," a former site of sun-god worship, that it has a pagan reference. Perhaps so. But God is sovereign over all, and because Samson's birth was a miracle and he had a Divine purpose, I think God influenced his naming. It was the dawning of a new day, a new sunrise. The Philistines would no longer be able to run roughshod over Israel. A brilliant, notched battlement was about to be introduced. And due to Samson' superhuman strength he was indeed a battlement, a fortification around Israel.

But before too long, Samson violated every vow of the Nazarite. First, he touched the carcass of a lion several days after he had killed it, violating his vow of never touching a dead body. On his way to Timnath, to visit a Philistine woman who had caught his eye, Judges 14:8-9 says, *"And he (Samson) turned aside to see the carcase of the lion: and behold there was a swarm of bees and honey in the carcase of the lion. And he took thereof in his hands, and went on eating, and came to his father and mother, and he gave them, and they did eat: but he told not them that he had taken the honey out of the carcase of the lion."* Why didn't he tell his parents where the honey came from? I think it's because he didn't want them to know he had broken his vow. In addition, they probably wouldn't have wanted any part of the honey if they knew.

Next, Samson took a Philistine wife. Judges 14:10 says, *"So his* (Samson's) *father went down unto the woman* (the Philistine woman to arrange the marriage); *and Samson made there a feast; for so used the young men to do."* That word "feast" here is *mishteh* and means, "drink, drinking, imbibe, drunk, banquet, feast." The implication is that he drank at their wedding feast. In fact, drinking bouts were common at Philistine weddings among the "young men."

But it would be the violation of the last Nazarite vow that would bring about his downfall. At this juncture his wife had been killed by the Philistines and he was now in love with Delilah who lived in the valley of Sorek. Judges 16:4 says, *"And it came to pass afterward* (after the death of his wife and his dalliance with a prostitute in Gaza) *that he* (Samson) *loved a woman in the valley of Sorek, whose name was Delilah."*

The Philistines had made several attempts to take Samson out but failed. Now, they saw their chance. Five Philistine lords approached Delilah, each offering her eleven hundred pieces of silver to discover the secret of Samson's strength.

This sum was too enormous to pass up and Delilah immediately went to work, begging, pleading, cajoling Samson to reveal his secret. Three times he lied. But the fourth time he finally told the truth. His power was in his hair. Wasting no time, Delilah cut off his seven locks while he slept, rendering him unable to fight the Philistines who came to subdue him. After that, they gouged out his eyes and put him in prison. It was a sad outcome for someone called by God before he was even born and who had been a judge in Israel for twenty years, (Judges 16:31).

But God was merciful and let Samson go out in a blaze of glory by pulling down Dagon's temple and killing himself along with more Philistines than he had ever killed throughout his life.

Samson was a mighty man of God, yet he failed. That word "Sorek" in Judges 16:4 is the only time it is ever mentioned in the Bible. Sorek means, "a vine, redness, yielding purple grapes, choice, tendrils." It also means, "hiss, whistle." *The Theological Wordbook of the Old Testament* page 957 says this about the meaning of Sorek: that hiss, whistle "often describes the reaction displayed by those who pass by the ruins of a once great city or power." How revealing!

How many mighty men of God have fallen after becoming enticed and entangled by an unclean thing? By evil associations? By their lust for money, fame, sex, or power and brough to their ruin? And after their demise didn't the world hold them in contempt for their failure and "hiss or whistle" at the wreck of a once great powerful man/woman of God?

But all believers, not only those in power or the limelight, should fear any unholy entanglements. We are not to love the world or the things of the world. 1 John 2:15 says, *"Love not the world, neither the things that are in the world. If any man love the world, the love of the Father is not in him."* And James 4:4 says, *"know ye not that the friendship of the world is enmity with God? whosoever therefore will be a friend of the world is the enemy of God."* And Romans 12:2 instructs us to *"be not conformed to this world: but be ye transformed by the renewing of your mind* (through God's Word, the Bible*), that ye may prove what is that good, and acceptable, and perfect, will of God."*

The Bible tells us there is pleasure in sin for a season, (Hebrews 11:25). So, yes, the things of the world can appear "choice" as well as captivating, until it does captivate and entangle us in its tendrils. Then misery and sorrow usually follow.

Oh, let us not enter the valley of Sorek. Let us not flirt with or dabble in those things forbidden by God because once we enter, a sad ending is assured. And touching the unclean thing can derail any ministry and hurt our relationship with God. Though God may show mercy, like He did to Samson, and still use us in some capacity, it is a chance not worth taking.

Valley of Berachah

This valley is in the Judean wilderness and the name "Berachah" means, "blessing". Let's see how and why the Israelites ended up here.

Jehoshaphat, king of Judah, was faced with an invading army of Moabites, Ammonites, and their allies, which 2 Chronicles 20:2 called a *"great multitude."* Jehoshaphat was a godly king who tried to turn Israel back to the God of their fathers. This coming attack was not the result of God's judgment, rather it was due to the hostility and animosity of those preparing to fight against Judah.

Fearing that Judah wasn't up to the task, Jehoshaphat petitioned the Lord and called a national fast. *"And Judah gathered themselves together, to ask help of the LORD: even out of all the cities of Judah they came to seek the LORD."* 2 Chronicles 20:4.

And God, in 2 Chronicles 20:15b, 17, answered by speaking through Jahaziel, whose name means, "beheld of God," and who was a Levite and descendant of Asaph, the psalmist. *"Thus saith the LORD unto you, Be not afraid nor dismayed by reason of this great multitude; for the battle is not your's but God's. . . .Ye shall not need to fight in this battle: set yourselves, stand ye still, and see the salvation of the LORD with you, O Judah and Jerusalem: fear not, nor be dismayed; tomorrow go out against them: for the LORD will be with you."*

God had heard their prayers. He had assured them of victory. The battle would be His. But before the battle began, Jehoshaphat reminded his army of God's promise. Then he ordered singers to go before them and sing praises to God. What happened next, according to 2 Chronicles 20:22, was amazing. *"And when they began to sing and praise, the LORD set **ambushments** against the children of Ammon, Moab, and mount Seir, which were come against Judah; and they were smitten."*

That word "ambushments" is *arab* in Hebrew and means, "to lie in wait, to lurk, ambush." But it was not the army of Israel that ambushed them according to 2 Chronicles 20:23-24. *"For the children of Ammon and Moab stood up against the inhabitants of mount Seir, utterly to slay and destroy them: and when they had made an end of the inhabitants of Seir, every one helped to destroy another. And when Judah came toward the watch tower in the wilderness, they looked unto the multitude, and behold, they were dead bodies fallen to the earth, and none escaped."*

Israel never fired a shot, so to speak. Rather, the armies of Moab and Ammon first turned on Seir, then on each other until they were utterly decimated. All that was left for the army of Israel to do was gather up the spoils. *"And when Jehoshaphat and his people came to take away the spoil of them, they found among them in abundance both riches with the dead bodies, and precious jewels, which they stripped off for themselves, more than they could carry away: and **they were three days in gathering of the spoil**, it was so much."*
2 Chronicles 20:25.

Then on the fourth day they went to the valley of Berachah to thank and bless the Lord (2 Chronicles 20:26-27) for this great victory *"for the LORD had made them to rejoice over their enemies."* They knew full well that their triumph had only come by God's hand. And what a thanksgiving celebration that must have been!

But it didn't end there. 2 Chronicles 20:29 says, *"And the fear of God was on all the kingdoms of those countries, when they had heard that the LORD fought against the enemies of Israel."*

What a marvelous story! And what a marvelous lesson! There are times in our life when we are called to stand in the gap for others or various situations, requiring intense spiritual warfare where we repeatedly go before the Lord or make continual declarations or are constantly binding and rebuking the devil. Sometimes these battles can last for years, as when a parent is standing in the gap for a child hooked on drugs or engaged in a rebellious lifestyle. But there will be other times when a strong enemy comes against us and after praying, fasting, and praising, God intervenes so quickly and so powerfully as to vanquish the problem completely, such as in an instant miraculous cure of some horrendous disease.

Just as king Jehoshaphat fasted, petitioned, and praised the God of the impossible, and never had to lift a finger in the battle but reaped the "spoils" of war, so at these special times we, too, will be kept from the fray and left to just reap the rewards. And when others hear of it, they, too, will have a reverential fear of the Lord and know that He protects and provides for His people. But these times should always end in the valley of Berachah where we thank and bless God for His greatness and mercy.

Oh, may we have a grateful heart and be ever thankful for all God does for us!

Valley of Dry Bones

The Valley of Dry Bones is an incredible place. It's where God took the prophet Ezekiel according to Ezekiel 37:1-14: *"The hand of the LORD was upon me (Ezekiel), and carried me out, in the spirit of the LORD, and set me down in the midst of the valley which was full of bones. And caused me to pass by them round about: and behold, there were very many in the open valley; and, lo, they were very dry. And he said unto me, Son of man, can these bones live? And I answered, O Lord GOD, thou knowest. Again he said unto me, Prophesy upon these bones, and say unto them, O ye dry bones, hear the word of the LORD. Thus saith the Lord GOD unto these bones; Behold, I will cause breath to enter into you, and ye shall live: And I will lay sinews upon you, and will bring up flesh upon you, and cover you with skin, and put breath in you, and ye shall live; and ye shall know that I am the LORD."*

These verses concern Israel, *"Son of man, these bones are the whole house of Israel,"* (Ezekiel 37:11). At that time, the Israelites were in Babylonian captivity. Their future looked bleak. They had ceased to exist as a nation. Essentially, they were "dead."

But God had other plans. Seventy years later they would return and rebuild their nation. Then in 70 A.D. when they were yet again decimated, God would once again raise up their "dry bones" by making them a nation in 1948, despite overwhelming odds.

Through restoring Israel, God has shown unequivocally that He can resurrect that which is lost, despoiled, destroyed, or brought down. But my question is this: if God can make a dead nation come back to life can He not make the dead things in our lives come back, too?

Many have, at one time or another, visited the Valley of Dry Bones. Maybe some of you are still there. Maybe your marriage is dead or your finances, or your job opportunities. Or it could be your good name, your reputation, your hopes, your dreams, all dead, all finished, or so you believe.

But remember, God is able to do *"exceeding abundantly above all that we ask or think"* (Ephesians 3:20). Dead marriages *can* live again. Our finances and job opportunities *can* change overnight. And hopes and dreams and reputations *can* all be restored. Nothing is impossible with God. But we must **BELIEVE** that God is truly able. That's the first step.

It's interesting that God asked Ezekiel to prophesy over the bones. I'm not a name-it-and-claim-it Christian, but I do believe in the power of prayer and the importance of speaking life (God's Word) over our situations. Therefore, the next thing we need to do is what Ezekiel did. We need to agree with God's Word and **SPEAK** it over our circumstances. In essence, we are prophesying over the dead things in our life with the life-giving Word of God thereby speaking life into them.

It's too easy to be negative and give up when we're in the Valley of Dry Bones. But if there is anything to take away from these passages in Ezekiel, it's that we shouldn't throw in the towel too quickly. We must resist the temptation to be negative. Speaking words of death while in this valley always leads to defeat. And in the end, we will get discouraged and give up.

So, remember two things are necessary if we want God to bring back these dead things in our life. First, we need to believe He's actually able to do it. Then, we need to act on it by speaking His word over our situation.

God's question to Ezekiel wasn't really a question. If God is involved, of course the answer to His question, "can these bones live?" is "yes"! And what of the answer to my question, can God "make the dead things in our lives come back, too?" That answer, also, is a resounding "YES"!

Valley of Baca

The Valley of Baca lies between Jerusalem and northern Palestine. Baca means, "weep, bemoan, make lamentation." It's the Valley of Weeping, a dry and desolate place. According to the *Pictorial Encyclopedia of the Bible* page 449, it's a "gloomy, narrow valley where brackish water trickles out of the rocks." It's not a place anyone would want to visit.

Yet, who has not passed through it at some time in their life? And that's just it. For me and those I know, it's only a valley that occasionally must be traversed. But what of those who actually *live* in this valley, who have lived in this valley for years or perhaps all their lives, and see no hope of ever getting out? I'm speaking of people far removed from my clean, orderly life; people I've read about or heard about in some documentary; people in third-world countries who forage in dumpsites to survive; children who have been stolen from parents and forced into the sex trade; people, like those in Haiti who, a decade after the 2010 earthquake that killed 300,000 people and left 2.3 million homeless, have yet to recover; people who have lost hope, who see no future.

It seems as if the scope of this valley is growing and may continue to grow in the months and years ahead. Floods, tornadoes, and hurricanes have already ravaged our country and countries everywhere. The homes of millions swept away, their life's work, their savings, gone. Countries continue to face financial ruin. And recently, food shortages and a pandemic have popped up. All grounds for weeping.

As the Valley of Baca enlarges and deepens, my prayer is that God will give those of us who don't live there, a heart of compassion, hands that seek to help, feet that run to comfort. The psalmist asked God to make the Valley of Baca for those going through it, a well, and rain to fill the pool. *"Blessed is the man whose strength is in thee; in whose heart are the ways of them. Who passing through the **valley of Baca** make it a well; the rain also filleth the pools,"* Psalms 84:5-6. Only God can fill such a dry and bitter place. Only God can give the needed strength to those who live there. Only God can fill those of us who don't, with the love, courage, strength and resources to make a difference for them.

Oh, may God give us His heart of love for those who weep!

Valley of Death

I'm a firm believer that as long as God gives us breath, we should appreciate our life and live it to the fullest for Him. But sooner or later, unless we are the generation that will experience the rapture, we *will* walk through the Valley of the Shadow of Death. Everyone dies. It's inescapable. While we needn't be morbid about it, we should consider what this event will mean in terms of eternity.

For a believer in Christ, that future is assured. Psalm 23:4 tells us, *"Yea, though I walk through the valley of the shadow of death, I will fear no evil: for thou (God) art with me; thy rod and thy staff they comfort me."* So, we are not to fear because God will be with us.

People tend to fear the unknown. But here, in verses 5-6, the unknown is made known, for not only are we told in verse 4 that God will be with us and comfort us, but now we see that He also has something wonderful waiting. *"Thou preparest a table before me in the presence of mine enemies: thou anointedst my head with oil; my cup runneth over. Surely goodness and mercy shall follow me all the days of my life: and I will dwell in the house of the LORD for ever."*

This describes a feast where God will anoint our heads will oil. A sign of respect given to an honored guest by his host, anointing one's head with oil was a common practice in Biblical times. It was mentioned in Luke 7, where Jesus was a dinner guest at Simon the Pharisee's house. While there, a woman with an alabaster jar anointed Jesus with its costly contents. As Simon watched, he became critical, thinking Jesus was wrong in allowing a sinful woman to touch Him.

Jesus, Who knows all our thoughts, immediately told Simon this: *"There was a certain creditor which had two debtors: the one owed five hundred pence, and the other fifty. And when they had nothing to pay, he frankly forgave them both. Tell me therefore which of them will love him most?"* (Luke 7:41-42)

Of course, it is the one who is forgiven the most who will love the most, and Simon gave the correct answer. That's when Jesus began listing the ways the woman honored Him, in stark contrast to Simon's lack of honor. *"Seest thou this woman?* (the woman who had come with the alabaster jar) *I entered into thine house, thou gavest me no water for my feet: but she hath washed my feet with tears, and wiped them with the hairs of her head. Thou gavest me no kiss: but this woman since the time I came in hath not ceased to kiss my feet.* **My head with oil thou didst not anoint:** *but this woman hath anointed my feet with ointment,"* Luke 7:44-46.

Jesus referred to three customary niceties a host offered an invited guest, none of which Simon did. The host greeted his guest with a kiss. Water was given for the guest to wash his feet because sandals were the shoes of the day and feet were usually dirty and dusty. And if the guest was important enough, the host would anoint his head with oil.

By God anointing our head with oil at the banquet, it says He considers us an honored guest. Also, the heads of kings and priests were anointed. And doesn't Revelation 1:6 and 5:10 tell us that God has made us kings and priests?

And then our cups will "run over," meaning we will never want for anything. We will have more than enough, and our blessings will overflow. And we will experience the goodness and mercy of God. Lastly, and most important-ly, we are promised that we will be with God forever.

Oh, what a future!

Thinking about this valley should do several things. It should remind us that life is brief and fleeting. Anyone over thirty knows how fast the days go. It should remind us that we have no guarantees about tomorrow or the next day. And because of that we should live our lives all out for the Lord and strive to finish our race strong for Him.

In addition, we should be concerned about the things of God which are eternal, rather than the things of this world which are fleeting and passing away. And thinking of this valley should also give us an incentive to **pray** diligently for those who God has placed in our lives because we know that they, too, must walk through this valley someday and that all eternity will be determined by what they decide about Jesus before they take that walk.

And finally, it reminds us that death is not the end, that we will be reunited with our saved family and friends who have gone before us.

Since this valley comes upon many people suddenly and unexpectedly, it is well to make sure we are right with the Lord. We will only pass this way once. And when it's our time to reach that shadowed valley, our houses, our bank accounts, our job titles will be meaningless. Only one thing will matter: "*Who do you say the Son of Man is?*" If the answer is "*My* Savior and God" we have nothing to fear, and unimagineable wonders await us.

But for those who can't answer that way, may you come to know the One Who died for you, Who sticks closer than a brother. The One who loves you like no one ever will.

Valley of Decision

It's not surprising that the last valley mentioned in the Bible is similar to the first two valleys in Genesis—the valley of rebellion (Shinar) and the valley of war and strife (Siddim). Like bookends, they tell us that man is incapable of governing himself or living in peace with others without God.

We come across this valley in the book of Revelation where it talks about Armageddon and what will happen there. Armageddon (Har-Megiddon) is the hill overlooking the Valley of Megiddo or Megiddone and means "to gather, or rendezvous." So, Megiddo is a place where, in the future, a gathering or rendezvous will take place.

This valley is also known as the Valley of Decision and Valley of Jehoshaphat—which means "God will judge." Beginning in the fourth century A.D. some claimed the Valley of Jehoshaphat was between Jerusalem and the Mount of Olives, which is currently a cemetery in a ravine. I don't adhere to that theory because it's hardly adequate for the nations of the world to gather. Whereas the valley of Megiddo is vast; a natural battleground that has been the site of dozens of armed conflicts over the centuries. It's the perfect gathering place where God will judge the nations. Both Joel and Revelation tell us why.

*"I will also gather all nations, and will bring them down into the **valley of Jehoshaphat**, and will plead with them there for my people and for my heritage Israel, whom they have scattered among the nations and **parted my land**. . . Let the heathen be wakened, and come up to the **valley of Jehoshaphat**: for there will I sit to judge all the heathen round about . . . Multitudes, multitudes, in the **valley of decision**; for the day of the LORD is near in the **valley of decision**."* Joel 3:2, 12, 14

"And he (God) *gathered them together* (for judgment) *into a place called in the Hebrew tongue Armageddon,"* Revelation 16:16. The nation's armies will gather here to destroy Israel; "to wipe it off the face of the map," or so they think.

Instead, God has allowed them to gather in order to render His judgment.

Revelation 19:11-16 tells what will happen. *"And I* (John, who was taken to heaven in Revelation 4:1 and given a preview of things to come during the seven-year Tribulation) *saw heaven opened, and behold a white horse; and he that sat upon him was called Faithful and True, and in righteousness he doth judge and make war. His eyes were as a flame of fire, and on his head were many crowns; and he had a name written, that no man knew, but he himself. And he was clothed with a vesture dipped in blood: and his name is called The Word of God. And the armies which were in heaven followed him upon white horses, clothed in fine linen, white and clean. And out of his mouth goeth a sharp sword, that with it he should smite the nations: and he shall rule them with a rod of iron: and he treadeth the winepress of the fierceness and wrath of Almighty God. And he hath on his vesture and on his thigh a name written, KING OF KINGS, AND LORD OF LORDS."*

When this occurs, the world will not only be against Israel but will be in rebellion against God and following the demonic leader the Bible calls "antichrist". God will judge them for both.

157

The battle will mark the end of this present age when Jesus returns to smite the nations of the earth, have the antichrist and his prophet thrown into the lake of fire, then separate the sheep (believers) from the goats (unbelievers), ushering in the millennial kingdom, the one-thousand-year reign of Christ. And it will be both terrifying and wonderful. Terrifying because God will destroy his enemies and their blood will reach the horses' bridles. And wonderful because He will usher in a thousand years of peace, harmony, and justice.

Events are already taking shape. Increasingly, the world is turning its back on Israel. World leaders have constantly pressured Israel to give up its land for peace. They have, in essence, tried to **part God's land**, and as a result will have much to answer for. But as global disruptions and financial disasters deepen, more and more people will be receptive to a world leader who promises to solve these problems, setting the stage for the antichrist.

So, are we marching toward the Valley of Decision? I believe so. And it could happen in our lifetime. But, praise God, we won't be here when that battle occurs. We'll be raptured beforehand. In the face of all this, it's time for the Church to rise up, to be strong in the Lord, to be the salt and light God meant us to be.

Sylvia Bambola

Author's Note

I think a good take-away from this book is that pain is universal, and no one will pass through life without experiencing some. Though each of our valleys will be different, it is evident that they, both the good and tough ones, are great teaching tools, able to stretch and strengthen us if we let them. And God allows all these valleys into our lives in order to make us a garden for His pleasure. That's the end game, to be His exclusive garden here on earth and then eventually in heaven.

But the first step is to come into the saving knowledge of Jesus. That means we confess we are sinners in need of the only Savior, Jesus. Then we ask Him into our hearts, give Him permission to take control, and endeavor to live the rest of our lives for Him. It's also important to read the Bible and connect to a good church.

For those who have never done this, may this be the first day of the rest of your life, living in the palm of God's hand and experiencing His incredible presence.

Love and blessings,

Sylvia Bambola
sylviabambola45@gmail.com

www.ingramcontent.com/pod-product-compliance
Lightning Source LLC
Chambersburg PA
CBHW061722020426
42331CB00006B/1045